INTRODUCTION TO THEOLOGY

THEODORE W. JENNINGS, JR.

INTRODUCTION TO THEOLOGY

An Invitation to Reflection
upon the Christian Mythos

FORTRESS PRESS
PHILADELPHIA

Library of Congress Catalog Card Number 76–007867
ISBN 0–8006–1234–5

5773E76   Printed in U.S.A.   1–1234

Contents

Preface

This book is an effort to answer the question: what is theology? That question has been raised for me in a variety of contexts but nowhere so urgently as when the responsibility of teaching theology was given me. Accordingly I am glad to acknowledge my debt of gratitude to those who have given the opportunity and challenge of teaching. Dean James T. Laney and Professor Theodore H. Runyon of Candler School of Theology first gave me that opportunity as a graduate student. The first course I taught (on the "Christian imagination") enabled me to begin the development of the ideas in the first half of this book. The invitation to teach at the Chicago Theological Seminary extended by then President Thomas Campbell and Dean Perry LeFevre to a young and, of all things, "Southern" theologian carried with it the obligation of teaching an introductory course in theological method which necessitated the further development of themes found in these pages.

I am also grateful to those who have read the manuscript at various stages of its development. In addition to the readers who remain anonymous I am glad to express my appreciation to Theodore Runyon, James Creech, and Ronna Case. They have not only read the manuscript and helped me to clarify the argument at a number of points but have also given me the constant support and creative confrontation which is the office of friendship.

The last two named were also, at much earlier stages, members of classes in which I attempted to work through these ideas. They are therefore exemplary of the numbers of people I have encountered in the classroom who have undertaken to be not passive recipients of instruction, but invaluable colleagues in the tasks of theology. Whatever merit this essay may have for students of theology is due to the penetration with which students and former students have struggled with me to make these thoughts clearer and more communicable. Whatever this text lacks in these qualities is a measure of how much more I have yet to learn from those to whom this work is dedicated—my students.

Chapter 1

Introduction

This book is an attempt to clarify the nature and tasks of theological reflection. Such a clarification is necessitated in the first place by the rather widespread confusion among students in seminaries and members of Christian communities generally about the character of this ancient discipline. At one extreme are those who suppose that any vaguely religious utterance may be understood as theology. At the opposite extreme are those who suppose theology to be the most arcane and esoteric of disciplines. My hope is to offer a description of theology which will enable the reader to understand something of the particularity as well as something of the breadth of this discipline.

Although I attempt here to describe the nature of theological reflection I cannot pretend to offer a neutral definition. This book is as much the communication of a personal vision of the theological task as it is a description and definition of that task as it has been understood for centuries. I am not, of course, of the opinion that theology is a discipline of my own making. In attempting to clarify its nature I have had to have recourse to the issues, perspectives, and descriptions offered as definitive of theology by a long line of theologians. I believe that my description and definition stand in some fundamental continuity with the way in which theology has been understood throughout the history of the Christian tradition—even at those points where my language and perspective seem most radically to diverge from those who have sought in other times to offer a description of it. Nevertheless the description offered in this essay is one which attempts to take into account a new situation for theology and to understand its nature and task from the perspective of that altered situation. Thus I have sought to situate theological

reflection within the broad cultural horizon which is designated by
the understanding of human being as *homo symbolicum*. I will be
concerned with illuminating that perspective and elaborating the
vision of theology which follows from it rather than being concerned with a recital of historical antecedents for the understanding
of theology herein presented.

The essay is an introduction in the form of an invitation. Part
of the malaise into which the study of theology has fallen in our
time is due to the fact that it is studied as something that other
people do and say rather than as a task which we too must and
may undertake. As an invitation to theological reflection, therefore,
the essay will attempt to point the way in which you may fruitfully
undertake the tasks of theological reflection. Only in this way
would it be possible to begin to understand the work of theologians
past and present.

In order to invite you to attempt to "do theology" it is necessary
to provide some guidelines for the performance of those tasks which
are theological in nature. In that sense this is an essay in theological
method. The definitions and guidelines which are offered here are
not intended to place restrictions upon reflection but are intended
to show that theology is a meaningful, helpful, and exciting enterprise. Thus, it is necessary in this introductory chapter to give
some advance notice of the way in which I understand the nature
and function of theology.

First, by theology I mean reflection upon the Christian mythos.
While much of the discussion to follow will seek to amplify and
clarify the meaning of the term mythos as it is used here, an initial
definition may be of some use to the reader. Mythos is used here
to designate that set of symbols, rituals, narratives, and assertions
which, taken together, announce and mediate the presence of the
sacred so as to represent, orient, communicate, and transform
existence in the world for a community of persons. The term
mythos thus designates a certain unity or structure in the religious
expressions of a people. The use of this term has the advantage
over the terms like story or narrative in that it points to the dimension of sacrality (there are a variety of kinds of story but only some
of them, presumably, are "religious") while including expressions
other than narratives (as, for example, ritual acts). The use of the
term is also an attempt to avoid the intellectualist bias of "world
view" and the privatistic bias of "faith." The argument of chapter

five will attempt to make clear the reasons for preferring the term "Christian mythos" to such possible alternatives as "kerygma," "gospel," "Christian faith," etc.

That theology is a reflection upon the Christian mythos suggests further that the term "theology" as used here will generally refer to Christian theology. I do not mean thereby to claim the superiority of Christian theology to all other varieties of theology whatever they may be. I do not see what could count for or against such a claim nor what it would mean should it be maintained or "proved." Still less is such a claim made implicitly or explicitly for the story upon which it reflects. Thus I claim only that my description of theology is adequate as a description of Christian theology. There may and indeed ought to be some applicability of what is said in this regard to the systematic reflection upon other religious stories but it falls outside the scope of this inquiry to elaborate them.

This preliminary definition does, however, serve to distinguish my view of theology from those who loosely employ Tillich to assert that any reflection upon issues of ultimate concern in existence is "theological." There is much that is appealing in that view for it cannot be denied that theology does indeed persistently and necessarily raise those questions. It is also true that such questions somehow fail to be raised and are even discouraged in other sectors of society and the university. It is characteristic of our time that questions of ultimate meaning for actual human existence are raised only or primarily in departments of religion and schools of theology. To many students these places, far from seeming to be the last bastions of medieval scholasticism they were once thought to be, seem instead to be the faithful remnant of truly humanistic inquiry. This reversal of roles is one of the genuine ironies of modern history. While I am strongly of the opinion that these departments and schools must continue to raise these issues in the broadest possible framework and not restrict themselves to a narrowly dogmatic or sectarian perspective (still less an excessively "professional" one), I am also persuaded that it would be a mistake to be seduced by this turn of events into abandoning the specific tasks and not illuminating the peculiar perspective of Christian theology.

This leads me to emphasize the character of theology as a humanistic discipline. It is an inquiry into the meaning of human life pursued by fallible human beings for whom the meaning of their own lives and that of their neighbors is at stake. Theology,

so long as it remains true to itself, is not concerned with endless
quibbles having no relevance to the living and experiencing of life.
The questions of human meaning are always raised by theology in
relation to its peculiar object, starting point, and perspective—
namely, Christian faith, Christian symbols, or what will be called
here the Christian mythos. This is so, not because of disdain for
other perspectives nor out of blind loyalty to tradition, but because
the theologian is persuaded that this perspective does significantly
illumine the character of human life in a way that is otherwise
missed or passed over by other disciplines. In this sense the task
of theology is undertaken on behalf of and for the sake of the wider
community of humanity and seeks to offer to that community an
interpretation of the world and human life determined by the
perspective of the Christian story. It is not the task of theology,
not even of dogmatic theology, to tell people what they must
believe or to impose by sleight of hand an ancient world view or
an arcane language upon an unwary public. Theological pronouncements derive neither from Olympus nor from Sinai as thunderbolts
from heaven but rather proceed from the earnest and open inquiry
of perplexed human beings who operate on the assumption (always
open to critical scrutiny) that decisive clues to the meaning of our
life on this earth are present in the Christian mythos.

This, of course, means that theology is an entirely secular, profane human discipline. This is something clearly recognized and
insisted upon by even a theologian like Karl Barth despite his
unearned reputation for a narrow dogmatism. But it is Bonhoeffer
who most emphatically asserts the worldliness of the Christian
faith, the Christian mythos, and consequently Christian theology.
How could it be otherwise with a story which has to do not with
God separated from the world and human experience, but with
God present as a human being in our world seeking to heal that
world and deliver it from bondage?

Precisely as this "humanistic" discipline of reflection upon and
articulation of the meaning of the Christian mythos, however,
theology stands in a peculiar relation to that smaller human community called the church. That relation is determined by the fact
that it is that community which attempts or claims to live out of
the Christian mythos. This does not mean that the theologian is
uncritical of the church or seeks to be its propaganda or public
relations officer in the university or some other setting. The service

which the theologian renders to the church is that of attempting to make clear its essential character as a community of the word. Here theology speaks with authority for it has the task of measuring the activity and speaking of this community against the mythos which is its ground. Without this service of critical theological judgment the church loses its way amidst the demands of institutionalization and the technology of program and expediency. That this last is largely the case in mainline Protestant churches in America shows clearly the paucity and timidity of relevant theological judgment.

The task of theology does not belong exclusively or primarily to the academic or professional theologian. It is the task of all clergy and laity who expect to exercise responsible leadership in that community and the task of all those who by virtue of their own needs, perplexities, and talents find themselves compelled to think through the basis and meaning of the Christian faith. Schleiermacher, in fact, tied the task of theological reflection directly to that of the exercise of leadership in the church. That relationship is sufficiently strong to make it the case that theology, insofar as it is taught at all, is taught in the seminary where Christian leaders are trained. This has had the unfortunate consequence of restricting theological training largely to members of the clergy. The opening of seminaries to those who do not expect to take on specifically clerical duties is a serendipitous occasion for the opening of theological training to a wider public—an occasion which may, however, be ruined by the move toward excessive professionalization of those very schools.

While professional theologians in an academic setting do have special training and responsibility for reflecting upon and clearly articulating the Christian mythos, they do not and cannot bear this responsibility alone. Too often theologians, like Boston Brahmins, speak only to one another. The dialogue which is the life blood of theological reflection requires that people in quite different contexts be involved in the tasks of theological reflection precisely in order to correct the excesses in aridity or insipidness which can characterize professional disputation. Karl Barth remarked that theological issues may be more acutely raised and receive more judicious responses in the catechetical classes of a country parson than in an upper level graduate seminar of the most prestigious theological faculty. I might add that in my experience there is often better theological reflection occurring over beer in some pubs than in many churches or schools of theology. It is indeed for such

people, clergy or laity, professor or student, that theology is a part
of the open, serious, lively, urgent, and joyful business of living and
seeking to understand life, that this essay is written in the hope that
theological dialogue, whether in the church or the university, will
increase in excitement, fruitfulness, and authenticity.

It is precisely to this end that I will attempt to suggest guidelines
for the doing of theology. They are not intended to serve as
shackles on reflection but rather as springboards for it, not to close
but to open up paths of exploration. I will attempt to show that
many of the odd ways of doing things which are peculiar to theology
are really common sense ways of pursuing its tasks and that, moreover, these methods provide useful insights for the prosecution of
any task which includes in its aim the uncovering of the meaning of
our common life. Traditional questions of authority, norm, and
source for theological reflection will be translated here into language
which attempts to reflect their actual basis in the human project of
discovering meaning and significance in life and history and community.

I will further attempt to show that these guidelines come quite
naturally out of the subject matter of theological reflection, namely,
the Christian mythos itself. That is, if our reflection is to conform
to the object of our reflection (one test of a "scientific" methodology) then certain ways of going about that inquiry necessarily
follow. Thus disputes about revelation and reason, Scripture and
tradition, logic and faith, or the authority of community or conscience derive directly from the nature of theology's preoccupation
with that peculiar subject matter called the Christian faith. Thus
methodological considerations will always be tied to both the
exigencies of reflecting upon human life and the peculiarities of the
Christian mythos.

I have introduced the word "scientific" intentionally and must
justify its use in this connection. What I mean to indicate by its
use in connection with theology is that theology is, in common with
a number of other human endeavors, involved in the practical task
of acquiring an understanding of our life and world. To that task
it brings a methodological rigor appropriate to its subject matter and
it is supplied with criteria whereby it is possible to separate knowledge from opinion, public from idiosyncratic. It is in this very
broad sense a science, not unlike history, literary criticism, ontol-

ogy, or ethics and shares these features at least also with the so-called natural sciences.

In calling theology a science I have no intention, however, of trading on the prestige of physics, chemistry, or biology. I only wish to draw the attention of my fellow students of theology to the presence of a certain methodological rigor in this field of inquiry which makes us responsible to one another in the rendering of clear, cogent, and one might even say, "correct" theological judgments. Theology is not or ought not to be a haven for all inarticulate sputterings about human life or Christian faith nor the sort of lunatic asylum where everyone does his or her own thing without facing the responsibility of giving an account for such speaking, writing, or gesticulating which is, or purports to be, of theological significance. I am, of course, not here counseling anything like orthodoxy but rather suggesting that a certain attention to questions of method may help to prevent us from confusing theology with woolgathering. I will have occasion, especially in Part II, to give some clues to ways of proceeding in reflection which introduce some rigor (but not, I trust, rigor mortis) into the process.

If theology is in some ways like a science, it is in others far more like poetry. It is really this latter—the relation of theology to the imagination—which is at the heart of the perspective which I will seek to elaborate.

PART I

THE "WHAT" OF
THEOLOGICAL INQUIRY

The first part of our task is to indicate the character of theology's object. It will be maintained that our object is a species of the fruit of imagination—that is, that theology reflects upon the Christian mythos which is itself a product of the human imagination representing the presence of the sacred in the world. This thesis will seem initially strange and radical and it does indeed derive, in part, from Feuerbach, but the course of the argument should indicate that it is not prejudicial to the truth of Christianity nor to the seriousness of theological inquiry nor to a doctrine of the Word of God. This thesis rather introduces, or seeks to introduce, clarity as to the task of theology by a more exact definition of the object of its reflection.

I will therefore first indicate the way in which the question of imagination arises as a key to an understanding of the theological enterprise. Then I will indicate something of the range of imaginative acts which lie at the basis of experience and culture, thereby filling out an understanding of imagination while at the same time indicating the place of religion in culture. I will then attempt an examination of the specifically religious imagination—its chief characteristics and types—and then try to show how the Christian mythos not only falls within this field but also entails a further specification of it. Finally, I will rejoin the question of the object of theological reflection by considering whether the view put forward contributes to more traditional formulations of the issue in Schleiermacher, Ritschl, and Barth.

I should perhaps say at the outset that the movement of the argument here is one which has so far proved itself useful to students of the most diverse theological opinions. It is meant to be neutral with respect to questions of theological content or doctrine though it arises out of one bias at least which may or may not be theological in nature—namely, that theology is a crucial and exciting task which has in common with other disciplines in the humanities the unremitting quest for the truth and meaning of our lives. The task of this first part is to indicate what sort of proximate ground it is that serves as theology's peculiar perspective on the basis of which to prosecute that task.

Chapter 2

The Imagination

This chapter will attempt an initial orientation to and understanding of the imagination. It will be argued first that modern culture has in various ways deprived itself of the imagination and that this deprivation has resulted in a critical impoverishment of human life and meaning. In the second section of the chapter it will be suggested that the imagination is that which mediates reality to reflection and thus grounds that reflection in existence. This will suggest then that the association of theology with imagination entails not a reduced but a heightened importance for the labors of theology. This will open the way to a consideration of the activity of imagination in the following chapter.

THE DISTORTION OF IMAGINATION

The imaginary stands in contrast to the real, the imaginative in contrast to the reflective. Into this context of widely shared belief and usage this essay introduces the thesis that theology has to do with a set of products of the imagination called myth and symbol. For some time Christian faith in particular and religion in general has been suspected of close alliance with the imagination, but the force of this suspicion depends upon the shady reputation of imagination. Something unconventional, untrustworthy, unpredictable, and therefore definitely unsavory and perhaps dangerous arrives on the scene. The association of theology with imagination can only be damaging to theology's reputation. Indeed the history of modern Western culture is in part the history of a struggle of those like Pascal, Herder, and Coleridge who have acclaimed the virtues of the imagination against the forces of what they have taken to be an increasingly narrow rationalism as represented by Descartes, Kant, Mill, or Comte. In the course of this long struggle, which continues to our day, the imagination has been largely relegated to the spheres of poetry and daydream. The consequence has been the emergence of what Owen Barfield has termed our modern "islanded consciousness."[1] That is, our awareness has largely been bereft of the imaginative faculty of sympathetic participation in the realities of life and world.

The emergence of science in the modern period brought with it a development in human consciousness which Theodore Roszak has labeled the "objective-manipulative consciousness."[2] A consideration of the excesses of objective and then manipulative consciousness will provide our first indicators of the loss of imaginative participation in reality. What is in view here is not the emergence of science or of modern philosophy as such but the attendant displacement of consciousness.

Objective consciousness

Objectivity has become the highest accolade bestowable upon thought. Contrary to some popular literature and some theological writing there is nothing insidious about objectivity as a goal of reflection. It is a description of reflection or inquiry which aims to reach a publicly intelligible and warrantable understanding of the world. But this entirely necessary and beneficial way of thinking may also become a way of living—the dominant mode of consciousness—and when this occurs we become cut off from the reality we seek to understand. We must briefly indicate why this is so.

The goal of objectivity, as that has been generally conceived, entails a movement of distancing of the knowing subject from the object of knowledge. It is an activity of separation. Now this movement of separation or distancing is quite complex. It is first of all a movement which attempts to eliminate the interference of bias, passion, willful or wishful thinking deriving from the subject. Thus the object must be disengaged or disentangled from this interfering subjectivity. The object is freed from contamination by the subject. Second, the movement of distancing posits an ontological and axiological chasm between the subject and object. The chasm is ontological in that two orders of being are posited—in Cartesian terms: *res extensa* and *res cogitans*.[3] The world of non-thinking matter is reduced to the status of "mere" object. It is there to be observed and described, not revered or communed with. But this movement of distancing recoils upon the consciousness of the subject. Consciousness must now conform to its object in such a way as to become, in that revealing phrase, the consciousness of the "detached observer."

Now when this model of consciousness is transposed in such a way as to function as the mode of being rather than simply a mode of thinking, the consequences are far-reaching. Reflection is now set at odds with the imagination. The imagination tends to hold subject and object together in contrast to objective reflection's demand for separation. In opposition to the demands of objectivity the imagination does not usually separate the emotional and passionate "how" of awareness from the "what" or object of awareness. In order, therefore, to achieve the distance necessary for objectivity the imagination must be suppressed. The more totalitarian the demand for objectivity, the more resolutely and completely must imagination be silenced.

To the suppression of imagination and the silencing of passion there corresponds the loss of the subject itself. This loss is the theme of Kierkegaard's polemic against the objective philosophy of the Hegelians.[4] Not that he supposed objectivity to be evil in itself but that its effects when applied to the existing subject were ruinous. It entails a denial of that passion wherein subjectivity and thus existence chiefly consists. The flight from the world of monastic, ascetic, or Manichean variety is replaced by a flight from the self. A flight which, to the extent to which it succeeds, is suicidal.

Corresponding to the loss of the subject there occurs as well a certain loss of the world. The world is constrained to conform to what is observable, calculable, predictable, quantifiable. There is no longer any sense in which self and world may be bound together with cords of mutuality and participation. The world becomes simply a machine whose mastery is within the grasp of the subject.

To the extent to which this becomes the habitual mode of consciousness, the "other" is similarly reduced and distanced. Persons, too, become objects of control and manipulation for the self that has learned to control itself and manipulate the world. The subject then is utterly cut off—from the world, from the other, from itself. The age of individualism dawns.

Manipulative consciousness

To this movement of objectivity there corresponds the ascendancy of the manipulative consciousness. This is the practical side of a theoretical objectivity. It involves the substitution of relationships of control and power for those of mutuality and participation. Bacon's famous dictum that "knowledge is power" has been verified beyond his wildest prophecies. The observation of the world facilitates human domination over that world. Indeed from the very beginning of the modern period the disciplines of objectivity have been linked to the rewards of power.

To a certain extent this may be seen to be inevitable. The wedge driven between subject and world by the objective consciousness makes of the "not-self" an altogether alien reality. That which is so utterly alien must be controlled and, indeed, in this controlling and manipulating of the object lies the chief distinction of the subject.

But to this control of the object corresponds control of the self. What must be suppressed or repressed in the self is all that may interfere with the efficient and calculating control of the object. As Hegel noted, the master is tied to the slave as the slave is tied to the master.[5] Relationships are reciprocal. The manipulation of the object entails manipulation of the self in order better to be the sort of self best able to manipulate the object. We are, in a word, well on the way to creating ourselves after the image of our machines.[6] To be sure, in the wake of Vietnam our attraction for self-images like James Bond may have at least temporarily waned. If our image of ourselves as efficient detached managers of the world is somewhat tarnished it has not yet been replaced by another. In the meantime the ethos of manipulative consciousness continues with barely slowed impetus to plunge ever further into what Jacques Ellul has called "the technological society."[7] In the society thus emerging the manipulative techniques have overridden all considerations of purpose and end. Persons are reduced to "useful members of society"[8] and relationships among them become conventionalized, compartmentalized, and ultimately trivialized. The nature for which we have long since lost any capacity for sympathy or mutuality in our headlong determination to use and dominate is disappearing beneath our garbage. With the severance of those intimate links to our world, to other persons, to our inner selves, we consign ourselves to an isolated autonomy wherein we must ultimately perish in the silent strangulation of our own humanity at the hands of our machines.

In some circles it is fashionable to lay this fate at the feet of reason—to make our rationality bear the blame for our madness. But reason too has been immeasurably reduced in the wake of our suppression of imagination. Reason is the steady orientation of the mind to reality. In its place have been set the various techniques of reason no longer subservient to reason's goal of understanding.[9]

The models of rationality which have replaced reason are many but a few of them may be indicated here. First, quantification has become a pervasive model of rationality and thus for reality. What cannot be reduced to numbers may seem increasingly unreliable and unreal. Moreover, the reduction of some issue or problem to statistical analysis may fill one with a heady optimism about its solution. The fate of such optimism as related to both war in Vietnam and war on poverty has become a part of our history, yet we are still assured that the computers bring us "not data (but) reality." There can be no question but that quantification has served as an immensely useful instrument of mind and culture and that it will continue to do so. But its displacement of the rather old-fashioned quality of wisdom in judgment is an impoverishment of reason itself.

Reason may also find itself reduced to literal and propositional assertions. Thus language is reduced to conventional assertions devoid of the nuance and passion which is more often suggestive of meaning than the literal and assertive proposition whose only merit is that it can be mechanically verified. When all truth is reduced to the single model of the literal and mechanically empirical then reality is truncated and reason correspondingly deformed.

Careful observation, cogently logical development, quantification, precise definition, unambiguous statement; these and more are the necessary and beneficent instruments of reason in its quest for understanding. But when reason is reduced to its techniques and the aim of understanding assumed or forgotten then reason loses its ground in human existence.

Islanded consciousness

Concomitant with the reduction of reason to its techniques and the ascendancy of the objective-manipulative consciousness has been the collapse of those primary symbols by which Western humanity has been sustained in its relation to cosmos, nature, and society.

The relationship between human life and the cosmic order was severed as the cosmos opened into the infinite and empty space of what we still call, euphemistically, the universe. As the near and harmoniously attuned spheres of classical imagination were replaced by the hurtling specks of cosmic dust we call galaxies, relentlessly receding through the void, the imagination recoiled from this alien and inhuman prospect. Nature too, as it was increasingly construed as a world of mechanism and determinism, seemed to become strange and alien. The sympathetic bond of organic unity was replaced by a mechanical necessity from which one must shrink like Descartes or Sartre or in which one could be ensnared as in the apocalypse according to B. F. Skinner. The French and Industrial revolutions conspired to bring in the wake of great benefits for human freedom and comfort a fresh loss—the loss of a sense of connectedness with society.[10] Instead of society and community there was now the state, the class, the crowd, the individual. Inevitably in existentialism and relational personalism the imagination withdrew into the sphere of the inward and intimate. But worst of all, we have lost touch with our own reality as we have attuned ourselves to the conventional and acceptable rather than heeding the persistent spontaneous images of dream and fantasy which mediate our interiority to awareness. Such at least is the conclusion of some like R. D. Laing[11] and Norman O. Brown[12] who have applied the insights of psychoanalysis toward an understanding of our culture.

The loss of the symbols by which we participate in the world of nature and cosmos, society and existence, results in the "islanding" of consciousness (Barfield). Instead of being sustained and connected by a web of meaning, modern consciousness seems increasingly separated, cut adrift, islanded.

These developments in our culture have been accompanied by a loss of respect for and solicitation of imagination. We have sought to substitute the literal for the symbolic, the objective for the subjective, the detached for the participatory. This was done in the name of increasing our humanity and has led to its impoverishment. The emergence of a counterculture has served to suggest that our impoverishment is greater than our affluence and that ways must be found to gain access once more to the wellsprings of reality and authenticity. That path lies not backward to some forgotten and now idealized era, but forward through a new consideration of and immersion in the human world of the symbol.

THE ROLE OF IMAGINATION

Having acquired some sense of the loss entailed by the ascendancy of the objective-manipulative consciousness and the collapse of symbols, we may now suggest a frame of reference within which to place this development. Early in this chapter I suggested that the modern period is characterized by the alienation of imagination and reflection. In the intervening sketch of the modern "islanded" consciousness we have noticed some of the consequences of this alienation. Already something of the place and significance of imagination has been indicated if only in the negative fashion of indicating the price of its loss. I must now attempt to describe the positive place and function of imagination.

Imagination is the initial way in which existence and reality come to expression in such a way as to be available to human awareness and to serve as the legitimate ground of reflection. This description will guide and summarize our argument.

Theology is often accused of being tied to an archaic three-storied universe. I will suggest a three-storied edifice of human experience. On the first or ground floor the paired terms "existence and reality" will be domiciled. The second floor will house the imagination and its product—the symbol. On the third will be placed reflection. The first and most important thing to be suggested by this model is that there is no direct or unmediated intercourse between reflection and reality. It is only by way of the imagination that access is to be gained to existence. This has several corollaries. First, the image or symbol produced by the imagination is the only way by which existence and reality come to awareness and thus become available to reflection. Second, that reflection which is alienated from imagination has lost its ground in reality and human life, and thus becomes empty, sterile, lifeless. Third, that reflection, insofar as it is wed to imagination, is to that extent grounded in reality. It should be clear that I have no intention of repudiating or limiting reflection as some champions of imagination have done, but rather to ground and enliven it.

Now let us examine this model more closely. It should be noted that existence and reality are placed here together. Indeed, at this level there is no disjunction between what we have learned to call subject and object, person and world. Existence is a part of the reality by which it is surrounded. In speaking of human existence we are using existence in a special sense which may be more precisely identified. A rock may be said to exist by which it is meant that it is *there*. A cat, however, may be said to exist only if it is not only *there* but also *alive*. Thus a dead cat which exists in the sense proper to the stone (it is there) does not exist in the sense proper to the cat (i.e., alive). The existence of a human being entails yet another level of the notion of existence. To speak of human existence is to speak of something more than a mere thereness or aliveness. It is this something more that is the subject matter, for example, of existentialist philosophy. What is entailed by the notion of human existence is a way of being in the world. It is a way of being characterized by participating in but also transcending the circumambient world. Thus it also refers to a peculiar structure of relatedness to the circumambient reality. It should be noted that often with good justification the peculiar structure of human existence is associated with awareness. The absence of awareness thus would mean the end of a specifically human existence. In the history of philosophy, however, awareness has come to mean the attention to clear and distinct ideas (thereby raising the questions of whether one humanly exists during sleep). For this reason, awareness, which dawns with the image, is omitted here from the definition of existence since what is in view here is the sense in which existence precedes and grounds imagination. *The function of imagination then is the representation of the patterns of participation in and transcendence of the world in such a way as to make possible the experiencing of, and conscious participation in, reality.*

We have said that imagination is the expression of existence and reality: it is as if through the imagination reality does indeed press itself outward and upward from darkness and silence into awareness. It is the force of this insistent pressure through the image that allows us to posit the real as the given which imagination molds to produce the image. The images thus created are an irrepressible and riotous collection: unicorns, atoms, trees, nightmares, apocalypse, utopia, and the heavenly hosts. They are vivid, sensual, emotive, and relatively undifferentiated. Reflection serves the task of distinguishing, ordering, and interpreting this world of images, thereby seeking to make more lucid the reality in which we live. In the performance of this task reflection does not replace or stand in opposition to the images it interprets but rather is itself engendered by them, guided by them, grounded in them, for through them reflection is related to the reality it seeks to understand.

This, at least, is how it ought to be. But when reflection is torn loose from the images and symbols which sustain it we are consigned to emptiness and isolation, and consciousness is impoverished and islanded. Then thought turns inward upon itself. No longer sensing itself to be derived from reality it seeks to dominate it. What an alienated reason is engaged in struggle with is not its death but its birth—it seeks to deny that it owes its existence to another (the imagination) and seeks to derive itself from itself. Thus it declares its absolute autonomy and thereby seals itself off from the life giving power of the image. The healing of reflection occurs by way of a return to the image. Such a return does not entail an abrogation of the role of reason but precisely its revivification.

We may consider the matter from another perspective. Given our model of the way in which reality is mediated by the imagination to reflection, we can see that even the objective manipulative and islanded consciousness of modern Western society must be itself based upon some selection of images which are taken to be the foundational presentations of reality to reflection. In the next chapter we will have to give some attention to the way in which images distort as well as mediate reality. In any case, the return to the symbol to which I have been pointing does not mean that no symbols are operative in a distorted consciousness, but that a selection of distorting images has been made and that in the name of such a selection the role of images and symbols generally has been denied. In this way an alienated reason attempts to deny its birth or origin. The appropriate response to this dilemma then is a reappraisal of the imagination and thus of symbols.

This reappraisal of the symbol–creating function of the human imagination is what Suzanne Langer[13] has called the new key into which philosophical questions are increasingly being transposed. The development of this new key, whose emergence can be assigned to no one thinker, owes much to the pioneering work of Ernst Cassirer whose monumental work *The Philosophy of Symbolic Forms*[14] has contributed significantly to an understanding of the range or scope of the field governed by and illuminated through a study of the symbol. Cassirer summarizes his thesis as follows:

> Between the receptor system and the effector system, which are to be found in all animal species, we find in man a third link which we may describe as the symbolic system. This new acquisition transforms the whole of human life. As compared with the other animals man lives not merely in a broader reality; he lives, so to speak, in a new dimension of reality.[15]

Cassirer accordingly proposes that the human being be defined not as an *animal rationale* but as an *animal symbolicum*.[16]

But in what does this activity of the symbolic system consist? Langer provides a useful analogy. The brain, she asserts:

> . . . is not merely a great transmitter, a super switchboard; it is better likened to a great transformer. The current of experience that passes through it undergoes a change of character, not through the agency of the sense by which the perception entered, but by virtue of a primary use which is made of it immediately: it is sucked into the stream of symbols which constitutes a human mind.[17]

This image of a transformer will inform much of our subsequent discussion. Following Langer we shall develop the thesis that the function of the imagination has great potential consequences for the future of culture. It promises to be the way to gain access again to those dimensions of reality from which we have severed ourselves. That hope and task is one in which many may share. The theologian has a particular concern here, for the task of theology consists in reflection upon the symbolic language of faith to the end of rendering it accessible for contemporary self-understanding. This task requires both an appreciation for and exercise of the activity of the imagination. If we are successful in showing that the object of theological reflection is a product of the imagination, we may also rescue theology from the inhibiting constrictions of a literalizing and reductionist approach to its task and open the way for an understanding of the way in which theology is also a quest for the significance of human life.

NOTES

1. Owen Barfield, *Saving the Appearances: A Study in Idolatry* (New York: Harcourt, Brace and World, 1965), p. 89.

2. Theodore Roszak, *The Making of a Counter-Culture* (Garden City, New York: Anchor Books, 1969). I am indebted to Roszak's analysis of contemporary consciousness at a number of points in this first section.

3. For a discussion of the impact of this "Cartesian dualism" in the history of modern thought, cf. Hans Jonas, *The Phenomenon of Life* (New York: Delta, 1968), pp. 7–25, pp. 58–63.

4. Kierkegaard's polemic against the Hegelians is scattered throughout his work, but the most important source in this respect is his *Concluding Unscientific Postscript*, trans. David F. Swenson and Walter Lowrie (Princeton: Princeton University Press, 1941).

5. Hegel's analysis of the "master-slave" dialectic is one of the most influential sections of his *The Phenomenology of Mind*, trans. J. B. Baillie (New York: Harper Torchbooks, 1967), pp. 229 ff.

6. L. Mumford, *The Myth of the Machine* (New York: Harcourt, Brace and World, 1967).

7. The most influential of Ellul's works is probably *The Technological Society*, trans. John W. Wilkinson (New York: A. A. Knopf, 1964).

8. Michael Novak deserves credit for pointing out the pervasiveness and perniciousness of this metaphor in his *Theology for Radical Politics* (New York: Herder and Herder, 1969).

9. The contrast between reason and technical reason is adapted from Paul Tillich, *Systematic Theology*, I (Chicago: University of Chicago Press, 1951), pp. 71 ff.

10. For an elaboration of this theme, cf. Robert A. Nisbet, *The Quest for Community* (New York: Oxford University Press, 1953).

11. R. D. Laing, *The Politics of Experience* (London: Penguin Books, 1967).

12. Norman O. Brown, *Life Against Death: The Psychoanalytic Meaning of History* (Middletown, Connecticut: Wesleyan University Press, 1959).

13. The argument of this section owes much to the work of Suzanne Langer, especially *Philosophy in a New Key* (2d ed.; New York: Mentor, 1962).

14. Ernst Cassirer, *The Philosophy of Symbolic Forms* (3 vols.; New Haven: Yale University Press, 1955). The first two volumes are especially relevant.

15. Ernst Cassirer, *An Essay on Man* (New Haven: Yale University Press, 1944), p. 24.

16. Ibid., p. 26.

17. Langer, *op. cit*; p. 46.

Chapter 3

The Range of Imagination

"The principle of symbolism with its universality, validity, and general applicability, is the magic word, the Open Sesame giving access to the specifically human world, to the world of human culture."[1] These words of Ernst Cassirer signal a new way of uniting the various fields of inquiry related to the study of the human world. It is within that general perspective which he was the first to elaborate that this chapter is located.

In the preceding chapter it was noted that imagination is to be understood as the principle and activity which mediates between existence and reflection. The activity of image formation, it was suggested, is far more definitive of human experience than the definition of the human being as a rational animal suggests. When the mediating function of imagination is severed then existence becomes mute and reflection empty. Thus what is at stake in attempting to recover the mediating function of imagination is a recovery of large dimensions of human life and meaning which become lost or distorted under the impact of what has been called the "objective-manipulative consciousness."

In the space which is available here it is not possible even to provide an outline of so large a task as that of the transformation or even understanding of human culture. What will be attempted, however, is a survey of some of the regions of experience within which we may discover important features of the activity of image formation, an activity which, following Suzanne Langer and Ernst Cassirer, we will call the symbolic transformation of the given. At the same time we will be suggesting the range of the field within which the object of theological reflection is situated. When the object of theological reflection and theology itself are placed within that field it should become evident that theology is in the true sense a humanistic discipline. The field is one governed by what

Langer has termed a new generative idea—it is the field of the symbol understood as the key to human consciousness and culture.

What is in view here may be designated as a convergence of quite disparate fields of investigation—the psychoanalytic interpretation of dreams, the advance of symbolic logic, the investigation of brain physiology, the phenomenology of religion, the existential ontology of Heidegger, the analysis of language in logical positivism, the emergence of the new criticism in literature, structuralist anthropology, quantum physics, the sociology of knowledge, surrealistic painting, and the new cinema. All of these and more converge in a major theme whose variations they each represent. That theme is the power, the structure, the refinement of the symbol.

I have divided this field into two segments—the general and the cultural. This division has only a provisional meaning—an initial and preliminary sorting out function. Under "general" I have grouped those acts of image formation which every normal human being performs daily and without effort. The general acts of image formation are those of seeing, dreaming, and speaking. Under "cultural" I have grouped those acts of image formation which require either a very high degree of specialization or which refer directly to social as opposed to individual acts of image formation. The cultural acts of imagination are to be discerned in the generation of science, art, politics, and religion.

What is in view here is not a general phenomenology of the imagination[2] but rather a survey of acts of the imagination. This survey serves two purposes: 1) to situate religious and the Christian imagination within the general field of imaginative acts, and 2) to provide an initial description of aspects of imaginative acts which will be of special importance for an understanding of the Christian mythos. The method here then is neither deductive (starting from the Christian mythos and then deducing the elements) nor inductive (beginning with a phenomenology of imagination as such), but somewhat more musical in that motifs introduced here are further developed in subsequent contexts leading to a kind of resolution in a consideration of the character of the Christian mythos.

GENERAL ACTS OF IMAGINATION

The three activities here designated as seeing, dreaming, and speaking seem at first to be quite simple. Yet they designate broad and inexhaustible fields of investigation. Seeing refers to the entire range of what is called sense perception, speaking refers to the phenomenon of language, and any discussion of dreaming immediately involves us in the whole range of psychoanalytic theory. Despite the enormous complexity underlying these simple words I will seek only to suggest a common structure to the activities thus designated.

1. *Seeing.* What is involved in the act called "seeing a tree"? I suggest that it is an astonishing feat of image formation. Here I will borrow models from physics and physiology to suggest the complexity and magnitude of that simple act.

Let us first consider a model derived from physics which pictures the antecedent conditions of seeing. This model has to do with light waves and force fields. According to this model the atmosphere of the earth is being bombarded with photons—bundles of energy—which derive from the continuous process of thermonuclear combustion in the sun. These photons are hurled at violent speed (the speed of light) from the sun onto the surface of this planet. Some of them smash into an object which we call a tree. At the level of physics a tree is constituted of atoms and molecules which are describable in terms of a complex energy field constituted largely of empty space and energy units or events named electrons, happening at a great relative distance from a center or nucleus. The photon strikes and is deflected from this energy field. Its rate and angle of deflection set up waves of light bouncing from the surface of the tree. The frequency of such waves and their strength constitutes the physical foundation of the act of seeing.

We turn now to a model derived from biophysics, biochemistry, and physiology. The light waves which are the product of the collision of photons with the complex force field called a tree collide once again—this time with the eye. Now to make a long and complex story almost childishly short and simple, we may imagine what happens in the following way. Simply put, the eye is being subjected to the virtually continuous bombardment of photons and is reacting to this bombardment. Its reaction is analyzable in terms of the reaction of nerve cells to the frequency, quantity, etc. of the photons striking them. Under impact these nerve cells discharge a small quantity of a chemical substance at the end of tiny fibers called axons. This chemical substance itself triggers additional nerve cells at their dendrite or receiving ends.

The bombardment of photons is translated into chemical reactions —physics becomes biochemistry.

The biochemical model must now be translated into brain physiology. In the brain there are 10 billion nerve cells. They are related by a complex chain of dendrites and axons—the tentacles of the various cells. Through this complex system patterns of excitation engendered by the message of the sensory apparatus emerge. These patterns are the moving waves of excitation racing through sets of neutrons coiling and looping through the reverberating system of the brain; the peculiar pattern and rhythm of this activity corresponds (by hypothesis) to the antecedent biochemical and physical data.

When we see a tree how does that happen? I have surveyed a few models which together provide a picture of the process which is prerequisite to that activity. But what has happened to the tree? Without the photons and their deflection we would not see the tree. Without the neurons, their sensitivity and discharge, we would not see the tree. Without the complex pattern of activity in the cerebral cortex we would not see the tree. But upon reflection it seems now more rather than less mysterious that we should see the tree. For when we see we do not see brain waves, neurons, light waves, photons, or force fields—but trees.

Or rather—we see an image of a tree. At the end of the process I have just sketched, the reverberating patterned discharge in the cerebral cortex is translated into an image with a precise shape, modulated color, shadow, and depth—in short, an image of a tree. Activity at the level of physiology and biochemistry is translated into an activity of conscious awareness. This last translation is what we call seeing. This translation is the most everyday act of imagination. But it is staggering in magnitude. Imagination has constructed (or re-constructed) the world—in this case the world of vision. Instead of force fields, photons, neurons, etc. we now have trees.

What is gained by this surrealistic plunge into the sciences of perception? First, we see what a significant alteration in the data is produced by image formation. If the immediate data of perception is the pattern of neuronal discharge in the cerebral cortex then the alien character of that designation to common sense already suggests the leap entailed in producing an image. Without that leap there is *no* perception, no human awareness.

Second, the image serves a function. We may describe that function as mediation between mind and reality. Image formation represents the world to awareness. It is the way the world is present to awareness. It is the access which the world has to the mind and the access which the mind has to the world. The relation of mind and world in the case of perception is not immediate at all, as we have seen. It is mediated by a series of translations, the last and most spectacular of which is that of image formation; without this complex of image forming activity there is *no* world and, conversely, no subject of awareness of that world.

The images refer to, designate, or represent a reality other than themselves. The images, surprisingly, do not refer to physiological operations of the cerebral cortex, nor to light waves. Rather they refer to trees, rocks, and buildings. We might be tempted to say that the images which we see really represent physiological processes going on in our brain or really refer to the impact of photons. But anyone who thought thereby to disclose the true significance of images would be forever running into—trees.

The images of perception are grounded in the physical, chemical, and physiological reality which provide the framework and foundation of the natural world. They refer to or designate the data in that reality. But they transform that data—transubstantiate it. Images are not photons (although photons are a kind of image). Despite the disparity between the image and the data it is only by courtesy of the image that the data is present to awareness.

We have spent so much time dealing with seeing for two reasons: 1) it is the most prosaic and everyday act of image formation and we are thus less accustomed to thinking of it in terms of imagination; 2) from this discussion have emerged themes which will be amplified by brief reference to other phenomena.

2. *Dreaming.* We will leave aside questions of its relationship via memory to perception. Here I will invoke the names of Freud and Jung to open up further dimensions of the activity of image formation. The achievement of Freud is not yet assessible if only because of its magnitude and yet untapped potential. But one thing which happens in Freud is that the rationalistic bias of our civilization is attacked at its root by one who was himself a thoroughgoing rationalist.

Perhaps that thesis of Freud which most sharply indicates his break with the prevailing rationalism of scientific inquiry is his dictum that "the unconscious is the true psychical reality."[3] This thesis, proposed in *The Interpretation of Dreams* (1900), summarizes the revolution in understanding which has produced the various psychoanalytic movements of our era.

The unconscious which is, of course, itself a symbol for a complex and largely unknown (and unknowable) reality may be penetrated by the understanding only in the most indirect fashion. By definition the unconscious is not directly accessible to the conscious operation of the mind. How then to gain access to the unconscious? "The interpretation of dreams," writes Freud, "is the royal road to a knowledge of the unconscious activities of the mind."[4] The statement that "the unconscious is the true psychical reality" was revolutionary; the proposal that science should concern itself seriously with dream interpretation was widely viewed as absurd. The interpretation of dreams, which, of course, is a very ancient discipline (take, for example, Joseph's interpretation of Pharaoh's dreams or Daniel's interpretation of Nebuchadnezzar's dreams) was largely the province of quacks and mystics. It was over against this widespread bias that Freud asserted that "dreams really do have a meaning and that a scientific procedure for interpreting them really is possible."[5] Against those who construed dreams as trivial activities of the brain, marking time during sleep, Freud asserted that "dreams are never concerned with trivialities," that dreams are not meaningless, they are not absurd . . . rather "they are psychic phenomena of complete validity . . . they are constructed by a highly complicated activity of the mind."[6]

Rather than permitting ourselves the luxury and delight of accompanying Freud along the royal road we must here keep to a few fundamental principles which will enrich our understanding of the symbolic transformation of the given.

First, we learn from Freud that a true understanding of our humanity is possible only by way of an investigation of the products of imagination, indeed by that most unruly, apparently insignificant, and often troublesome of imagination's offspring—the dream.

Second, we learn that the reality to which we thus have access is otherwise hidden from view, cloaked forever in the inchoate silence of repressed desire. Apart from its image, that reality—the true psychic reality—is closed to the prying eyes of consciousness.

Third, we learn that the reality transformed by those images is altered, distorted, and abridged in that process of imaging. The dream which reveals also conceals. It is not a direct transcription of that reality from which it springs but is a text coded, edited, and displaced.

Fourth, we learn that despite the arduousness of the task of interpretation—which is a reflection upon those images—it is a task which must be prosecuted radically and faithfully if we are to achieve that modicum of sanity whose only alternatives are an impoverished and isolated rationality or madness.

As is well known, Freud discerned in the dream the representation of the childhood of desire. Jung discovered there also the childhood of the human race. Freud saw there the dynamics of repressed desire; Jung also saw there the source of healing, integration, the path to wholeness. Again only a few principles must suffice to represent the wealth of potential understanding which opens here to view.[7]

First, in the images produced with such apparent abandon by the unconscious, Jung discerns those archetypal images which serve as the basis of myth and dream alike. That is, the symbols recapitulate the experience and wisdom of the entire human race. The unconscious is also a collective unconscious.

Second, the reality to which we thus have access is not only the specific dynamic of our life history but is also the generic pattern of our common humanity.

Third, the aim of such symbolization is the growth, transformation, and healing of the human being. This is a notion of major importance for it suggests the teleological character of symbol formation which is not simply a reporting of but also a summoning to reality. This therapeutic function of the symbol suggests a way of healing the damage done through the truncation of our experience and anticipates what shall be said subsequently about the religious imagination and reflection upon the Christian mythos.

Fourth, the dream image is not reducible to simple truths about life but is in its density, variety, and sensuality the most adequate language in which to express its meaning. The task of interpretation is therefore only to make us attentive to the image, never to make the image unnecessary.

In looking at dreams the notion of symbolic transformation has been broadened to include not only perception but also desire, not only waking but also sleeping, not only the outer world but the hidden world as well.

3. *Speaking.* With the act of speaking we become human. Here I will not attempt an analysis of that activity but only point to the way in which language is itself the transformation of reality into a world of sign and symbol which presides over both waking and sleeping. At bottom all discussion of imagination is an analysis of language. Even the unconscious, as Freud maintained, is structured like a language. If we speak here of imagination rather than language it is only because at the end of our road is a recovery of a sense for language which is not immediately open to us since we have lost a direct appreciation for its representational, symbolic, and mythic power.

It has become customary over the few centuries of the modern period to associate language with a theory of perception. In that case language is taken to be simply the naming of perceptual image. However, language, as will become especially clear in the case of religious language, is not reducible to a simple process of naming. Structural linguistics, for example, is making increasingly clear the way in which words do not simply name a non-linguistic reality or image, but rather designate a nexus of relationships within the nexus or structure of language itself.[8] Some kinds of hermeneutics are emphasizing the way in which language actually evokes and conveys the interiority of the speaker rather than having to do primarily with the world out there. Moreover, a rhetorical analysis of language would emphasize that the verbal meaning has far more to do with the hearer. This array of complex analysis of language suggests the complexity of the phenomenon—a complexity far exceeding the capacity of an analysis which functions on the naming model to account for. When to this is added the fact that language, far from being passive with respect to existence and world, actually shapes, directs, and limits even sense perception, then it becomes manifest the degree to which the realms of what we are calling the symbolic transformation of the given and that of language itself are very nearly coextensive.

Although we cannot stop here to discuss language we may note that its very mention drives toward an investigation of the cultural acts of imagination. Unlike seeing and dreaming, speaking is something with which we must struggle consciously in order to learn to do it. Since it is universal it seems that it is derived from nature, but because it requires learning, it is already a cultural reality.[9] It is the point of intersection between the realm of nature and the realm of society. In it we are already in culture.

CULTURAL ACTS OF IMAGINATION

The temptation is to believe that imagination is a purely individual activity and therefore subjective in the sense of being private and idiosyncratic. It is this notion which has been used largely to discredit imagination as being restricted to the purely private sphere of individual eccentric mental states. This notion is even approved of and emphasized by those who celebrate the imagination as the last bastion of individuality and inwardness. To be sure, imagination bears a remarkably personal stamp. But only the peculiarly modern disease of absolute isolation could bring us to conceive of persons as atomistic and autonomous monads without interior connectedness. It is only such an atomistic view of human life which could lead us to suppose that anything appropriately human such as imagination could be individual in the sense of atomistic subjectivity.

Already in giving attention to the general sphere of acts of image formation it should be clear to what extent the act of image formation is a social act. Of course, with language it is obvious that we are in the presence of a social phenomenon. But even in the case of dreaming we are already engaged in a social process with roots deep in the collective unconscious of the human race. This is already suggestive of the non-atomistic character of human imagination.

Those cultural achievements ordinarily designated as works of artistic genius further clarify the intersubjective character of imagination. The poem, the painting, the statue, the symphony: all are products of a personal imagination stamped forever by the peculiarities of their creator—yet they are also of a universal and abiding power. It is of their very nature that they communicate to people who had no part in their making, arousing in the mind of the beholder those resonating vibrations—sometimes dim, sometimes overpowering—of significance, import, and mood. We may not pause here to investigate the way in which this happens or the structures of imagination which make it possible. That it happens at all shows that we are more deeply related to one another than we allow for in our cultural ideologies of individual atomism. The most intensely personal visions of the artist or poet forged in the crucible of intimate anguish and private ecstasy are precisely those most evocative of our response and recognition. Works which bear no such personal stamp we dismiss as banal, commonplace, or even unimaginative. It should be clear then that what emerges from the imagination is not restricted in significance to the individual. Imagination is subjective in the sense that it proceeds out of the subjectivity of imaginative creation and resonates in the sympathetic imagination of another's subjectivity—but it is, for all that, a social act.

Accordingly, when we speak of the imagination as well as of its artifacts it should not be supposed that we are speaking of something that has to do merely with the individual's private fantasies. We are speaking of that power of human being which is both personal *and* universal, intimate *and* social.

It should not seem strange, therefore, to speak of the role of imagination in our political and social life. Human community arises from and is sustained by the political and social imagination. Without the operation of that imagination human community would be impossible for the deceptively simple reason that it would be unimaginable. The cohesion of the group (without which human life is impossible) derives from mutual participation in shared images, symbols, and in the narratives and principles which elaborate them. Among primitive peoples, those living at the dawn of history or on the edges of contemporary civilization, we find taboos regulating communal behavior, symbols of authority, and legends concerning the peculiar origin and character of the group. In societies primitive or otherwise these images and narratives bring social experience and existence to expression; without them that social life itself disintegrates. What I would call the autonomous function of political imagination is the elaboration of images and symbols which create and sustain the identity and cohesion of the society.

Just as the imagination of the individual may become diseased and distorted—creating a symbol system which denies rather than expresses the identity of that person—so also may the images and symbols of society become a false consciousness which distorts the human reality they purport to express. This is the heteronomous function of political imagination. It may be that these images once did but no longer do correspond to the social reality. They now only serve the interest of particular groups. They are perceived not as bringing to expression the authentic aspirations and relations of a society but as imposed by the rulers who now manipulate these images to their own ends or as imposed by the dead hand of the past whose cadaverous representatives exercise authority amidst the odor of sanctity and decay.

A third way in which the political imagination may function is teleologically. Here we have images which do not correspond to a present reality but which envision a future reality upon which model the present is to be fashioned. Here are the myths of utopia and the eschatological hopes of the left wing Reformation or Marxian vision. The conjunction of a theoretical utopianism with a Christian millenarianism has produced our modern history of revolution.

From this all too brief catalogue of socio-political imagination two principles which will recur later have emerged. First, the images and myths created by imagination sustain social life. Second, the images thus formed may express, distort, or seek to transform the reality which they purport to represent. With appropriate qualifications these principles also govern the entire field of image formation.

No brief survey of the field of the function of imagination in culture would be complete which omitted what we have grown accustomed to designate as the sciences. Science in the narrow sense includes the physical sciences primarily and secondarily some forms of psychology and sociology. Imagination plays several crucial, though until recently often unnoticed roles in the activity of the scientist. In *The Structure of Scientific Revolutions* Thomas Kuhn[10] has explored the fundamental importance of the paradigm which serves as the fundamental and guiding image for the work of the scientist. Examples of such paradigms are the Copernican heliocentric system, the Newtonian model of mechanics, and the relativity theory. The paradigm becomes the picture of the world or of some region of reality which it is the task of the scientist to elaborate in accordance with mathematical and experimental methods. This is a sort of mopping up operation which further articulates all applications of the theory derived from the paradigm. The paradigm and the theory which is derived from it serve to define what counts as a legitimate problem for investigation. Now what is crucial is that the paradigm itself is neither derived from nor verified through a direct observation of nature. As has been shown in Arthur Koestler's *Act of Creation*[11] and in other similar volumes, the paradigm of theory is discovered very often through a dramatic leap of imagination which succeeds in picturing the field of inquiry differently. Moreover, should such a paradigm succeed in gaining acceptance it is not, as Michael Polanyi has shown, on the basis of supposed evidence but rather on account of what may be called the aesthetic qualities of the paradigm (simplicity, suggestiveness, harmony, etc.).[12] Further, as both Polanyi and Kuhn have made clear, the paradigm creates and defines the community of relevant scientists; it becomes a social definition of reality.

It should be noted here that in the description of perception with which the chapter began, the discussion was based upon a series of such paradigms or images no one of which is more real than the others but each of which describes the world through the image which constitutes it as a science.

The scientific imagination then is a crucial constituent of our culture with its own contribution to make to the notion of image formation. With a consideration of science we see how an image has an *exploratory function*. That is, it serves to guide inquiry as well as to represent reality and define the society of scientists. This suggestive and exploratory character of the image is crucial for poetry and religion as well as for science.

Special consideration has been reserved for mathematic and quasi-mathematic (e.g., symbolic logic) symbols. Because of their lack of concreteness they differ greatly from most other kinds of symbols though they do display a range of imaginative functions. It is worth remembering that mathematics originates, in the West, in the context of a mystical ascetic religious community called the Pythagoreans after their shadowy founder. The peculiar power of numbers to be passive of any content and thus to link all kinds of content stirred then as it has since a religious awe. Two stars, two stones, two eyes—apparently quite disparate yet linked together by the power of the number. Moreover, the numbers may be freed from association with any content whatever and enter into relations with one another by addition, subtraction, multiplication and division. Surprising relationships may emerge. One that seems to have awed Pythagoras himself was the relationship between the length of a pipe and the sound it made—thus quantity and quality enter curious union.

Here we have displayed several important features of the symbol. First, the symbol provides a way of relating diverse dimensions of our world—a link between otherwise disparate and
opposed fields of experience. Second, the symbol provides a way
of organizing and ordering such ranges of experience by introducing into them a comprehensive structure of general categories, thus
freeing attention from the sheer random multiplicity which would
otherwise overwhelm it.

We may conclude this discussion of the cultural activity of
imagination with some brief remarks about philosophy. Philosophy, in its broadest sense, may be understood as the systematic
reflection upon all the regions of image formation we have specified.
Increasingly the tasks associated with this reflection have become
so specialized and the data upon which reflection proceeds has
become so enormous in scope and complex in detail that the various
sciences and humanities have gradually become entirely autonomous
disciplines. The chief residue of a broad conception of the philosophic task is the custom of granting a Doctor of Philosophy degree
to those with the highest level of formal training in fields as varied
as chemistry, history, and religion. The assumption reflected in
this custom is that these persons are not simply practitioners of a
technique but also involved in the task of systematic reflection
upon that field in its particularity and its relationship to other fields.

Under the influence of figures as diverse as Cassirer, Wittgen-
stein, Russell, Heidegger, and Ricoeur, philosophy is increasingly
hearing the summons to a reflection upon the linguistic and symbolic character of human experience. This is not, as some have
supposed, a counsel of retreat from its traditional preoccupation
with questions of ontology and epistemology. As Plato was the
first to see clearly, the question of being is one which is intimately
and fundamentally bound up with what we today may call the
linguisticality of our existence. In the summons to become a
philosophy of culture or a comprehensive hermeneutics (Ricoeur),
philosophy is being summoned to take up its ancient task of a
comprehensive reflection upon the field of the symbol. In a subsequent chapter we will discuss the relationship between theological
and philosophical reflection.

This brief survey should give us a clue as to the wide ranges
constitutive of the field governed by the symbol, but it can serve
only as the barest indication of its complexity and variety. In each
of the ways indicated the imagination—so often associated primarily

with fantasy and fiction—plays its irreplaceable and foundational role mediating the reality of world and existence to awareness and reflection. This is not to dissociate imagination from fantasy, for there is in all of these activities of imagination, whether in scientific theory, utopia, dream, or calculus, the same quality of creative activity and playful "as if" quality which characterize the works more usually associated with imagination. Indeed the entire field of human experience is dominated by the play—now serious, now frivolous—of the imagination which introduces into all of experience a certain element of whimsey and grace which may be systematically ignored but never entirely suppressed. This is why it is not far-fetched for a philosopher like Ernst Bloch to take fantasy to be the key to an understanding of human being.[13]

We may now summarize the characteristics of the image or symbol as suggested by this overview of the field of imagination. First, in our discussion of perception we noted the great leap which is involved in the transformation wrought by the imagination upon its given in order to produce even the simplest perceptual image. We also discovered the way in which the image serves to represent reality—a reality which, as is especially clear in the relation of dreams to the unconscious, is otherwise completely inaccessible. The practical and irreplaceable function of the image or symbol is that it provides the only access to reality. But it is not a simple representation of that reality. In the space of that great leap separating the image from the data upon which the imagination worked its creative will, there occurs a fundamental transformation. This transformation is an alteration which may distort and conceal as much as it makes manifest. This is what Freud noted in the case of the dream and what, in social reality, has been called by Marx and others "ideology." It is also here that we could place the origins of the distorted consciousness which was examined in the second chapter. This same activity of the transformation of the given, however, may function teleologically to heal or improve. Thus, we have seen what Jung calls the "symbols of transformation" and what we have called the teleological or utopian functioning of imagination in the area of society and politics. As we also noted in the case of the political imagination, the image or symbol may actually serve to create and sustain the human reality which it represents, that without its operation, community and communication in their human form could not exist.

We have also noted the social character of imagination. It is not to be limited to the strictly private and idiosyncratic but as we have said, creates and sustains the public and social world of human culture. Even in the dream we have seen, following Jung, the deep interconnectedness among human beings which sustains and fashions the most apparently idiosyncratic productions of the imagination. Owen Barfield has noted the way in which even our perceptual images are collective, that is, partially determined by the language and shared preconceptions of our society.[14] This collective, public, and objective character of the image does not stand in opposition to the subjective, for as we noted in the case of artistic creation, the passionately personal and the universally recognizable converge in intimate union.

The case of mathematics has suggested the function of the symbol to unite otherwise disparate objects and levels or dimensions of experience. This ability, when coupled with the exploratory character of the symbol (as with the paradigms of science), makes clear that the image does not deliver to us its given—signed, sealed, and packaged—but serves as the impetus toward reflection and elaboration.

That is to say, with Paul Ricoeur, that "the symbol gives rise to thought."[15] Far from being the opposite of reflection or a holiday from it, imagination is that without which reflection is sterile, empty, and ultimately impossible. It is not because of an excess of reason but because of a paucity and obstruction of the imagination that we have witnessed the ascendancy of the objective-manipulative consciousness. Only when reflection becomes itself thus impoverished and warped does it stand in opposition to the creative and spontaneous life of the image.

NOTES

1. Ernst Cassirer, *An Essay on Man* (New Haven: Yale University Press, 1944) p. 3.

2. Among the phenomenologies of imagination which are the most interesting and helpful for the theologian are Ray L. Hart, *Unfinished Man and the Imagination* (New York: Herder and Herder, 1968) and Karl Rahner, *Spirit in the World*, trans. William Dych, S.J. (New York: Herder and Herder, 1968). I found the first of these especially helpful.

3. Sigmund Freud, *The Interpretation of Dreams*, trans. James Strachey (New York: Avon, 1965), p. 651.

4. *Ibid.*, p. 647.

5. *Ibid.*, p. 132.

6. *Ibid.*, p. 215.

THE "WHAT" OF THEOLOGICAL REFLECTION

7. For further elaboration of Jung's view, cf. *Two Essays on Analytical Psychology,* trans. R.F.C. Hull (Cleveland: Meridian Books, 1956), and *Man and His Symbols,* (New York: Dell, 1968).

8. For those interested in an introduction to structuralization, it would be useful to examine a book such as *The Structuralists from Marx to Levi-Strauss,* ed. Richard and Fernande DeGeorge (Garden City, New York: Anchor, 1972).

9. For a discussion of the relationship of nature and culture, cf. Claude Levi-Strauss, *The Elementary Structure of Kinship,* trans. J. H. Bell revised edition (Boston: Beacon Press, 1969) pp. 3–11.

10. Thomas Kuhn, *The Structure of Scientific Revolutions* (Chicago: University of Chicago Press, 1962).

11. Arthur Koestler, *Act of Creation* (New York: Dell, 1967).

12. Michael Polanyi, *Personal Knowledge* (Chicago: University of Chicago Press, 1959).

13. Ernst Bloch, *Das Prinzip Hoffnung* (Frankfurt-am-Main: Suhrkamp Verlag, 1959); excerpts from a range of Bloch's writings are more readily available in *Man on His Own,* trans. E. B. Ashton (New York: Herder and Herder, 1970).

14. Owen Barfield, *Saving the Appearances, A Study in Idolatry* (New York: Harcourt, Brace and World, 1965).

15. Paul Ricoeur, *The Symbolism of Evil* (Boston: Beacon Press, 1969), p. 348. This essay as a whole owes a great deal to the pioneering work of Ricoeur in developing a hermeneutic of symbols. While his position is not yet finalized, the reader should consult *Freud and Philosophy: An Essay on Interpretation,* trans. Denis Savage (New Haven: Yale University Press, 1970), and also consult the journal *Philosophy Today,* XVII, No. 2/4 (Summer, 1973), which contains several more recent articles relevant to the question of understanding symbolic language.

Chapter 4

The Religious Imagination

In this chapter I will give some consideration to the question of the character of religion, accepting Feuerbach's thesis that the imagination produces the myths and symbols which characterize it, and accepting as well the thesis of Eliade (and others) that it is the sacred in conjunction with the human world which is the "given" for the religious imagination. It will then be necessary to investigate the nature of the religious symbol, bearing in mind what has been learned in the preceding chapter. The chief modes of the religious imagination will then be considered. Finally, the various functions of the religious imagination will be specified completing the discussion of the religious imagination and preparing the way for a consideration of the Christian imagination.

RELIGION AND IMAGINATION

That an inquiry into the foundation of theological method involves a consideration of the nature of religion generally is an insight which was first truly made into a methodological principle by Friedrich Schleiermacher[1] who is also justly named the founder of modern theology. Throughout the nineteenth century this remained a significant feature of theological inquiry, though it was also regularly accompanied by the apologetic motive of showing that Christianity was the absolute, final, or highest form of religion. In the twentieth century, however, this concern has largely diminished owing in part to the influence of Karl Barth's thesis that Christianity is not a religion at all, and to the increasing specialization of the disciplines relating to the study of religions. Of major twentieth century theologians, Tillich alone seems to have grasped its true importance only toward the end of his career.[2]

The nineteenth century witnessed considerable scholarly advance in the study of religions, especially what was then called "primitive religion." The study of the presumably less developed religions bore with it the temptation to speculate with respect to the origin of religion, producing some rather fanciful speculation which we read today with a touch of amusement. One of the first of these views is that of E. B. Tyler who suggested that religion springs from a childlike inability of the "primitives" to distinguish waking and sleeping states, leading them to populate the former with the phantasms of the latter.[3] Perhaps the most famous of these scholarly attempts to create its own "myth of origin" is Freud's tale of the "primal horde."[4] Nevertheless, some very important insights do emerge in this period, especially two derived respectively from Feuerbach and Durkheim.

It is Feuerbach who deserves credit for first developing the thesis that imagination plays a decisive role in the formation of religion. Unfortunately, Feuerbach is too rarely studied by theologians and usually assumed to be yet another of those "despisers of religions" with little to contribute in a positive way to an understanding of theology's task. Only Barth has taken the trouble to commend him to the attention of theologians generally—something he would not do even for his great predecessor, Albrecht Ritschl.[5]

The crucial argument, for our purposes, is contained in the twentieth lecture of Feuerbach's *Lectures on the Essence of Religion*. Here is a fragment of his argument.[6]

> I do not deny religion. I do not deny the subjective human founda-
> tions of religion, namely feeling and imagination and man's impulse
> to objectify and personify his inner life, an impulse which lies in
> the very nature of speech and emotion, I do not deny man's need
> to lend nature a human aspect . . . I do not deny his need to con-
> template nature in poetic, philosophic and religious terms. I merely
> deny the object of religion or rather of religion as it has been up to
> now. I should merely like man to stop setting his heart on things
> which are no longer in keeping with his nature and needs and which
> he therefore can believe and worship only by coming into conflict
> with himself.

This much illumines for us Feuerbach's intent which was not to deny the religious need or sense of humanity, but rather to assist us in reclaiming the religious as part of *our* nature rather than as something having reality apart from us and in conflict with us. Religion, he is maintaining, springs from human beings and is expressive of their greatest aspiration and of their own essential

nature. But in religion, "as it has been up to now," this human
basis is objectified—given a reality independent of our own and
thus we lose a part of ourselves, that is, we are alienated from
ourselves. In order to rectify this alienation Feuerbach attempts
to show that: "the theoretical cause or source of religion and of its
object, God, is . . . the imagination."[7] We should not be surprised
to hear Feuerbach go on to say that "A God is an imaginary being,
a product of fantasy."[8] What may be surprising, however, is to
learn that Feuerbach gives the credit for the key insight in his
position to none other than Martin Luther. Feuerbach's phrase:
"God does not exist in sense perception or in reason but only in
faith, *that is, imagination*,"[9] is meant to be reminiscent of Luther's
famous dictum in the Larger Catechism: "that upon which your
heart depends, that is your God." This same thesis of Luther's
was developed in a different context by Feuerbach's contemporary,
Søren Kierkegaard who, in similar fashion, emphasized the subjective character of faith (the how) in contrast to its object.

Now the point of this is not to lay claim to Feuerbach's so-called
reductionism but to emphasize as he did that, whatever we may
think of their truth or falsity, the myths, symbols, and dogmas of
religion are creations of the human imagination. This position
does not entail atheism as Feuerbach seems to have thought.
Instead it represents the rather commonsense insight that whether
the ultimate source of religion is God or human aspiration or
human misery or what have you, it only comes to expression in
human speech and symbol.[10] This is not to deny some objective
reality to God but only to say that whatever God (or faith) is in
itself, it is present to reflection only as already represented—that
is, as mediated by the myths and symbols into which whatever
reality may lie behind them has already been transfigured. Our
early discussion of the symbolic transformation of the given as the
fundamental character of imagination comes now to our aid if we
remember that the only access to reality is by way of the image
which both mediates and transforms that reality but is not that
reality itself.

The question may justly be raised, however, what is that given
that is thus represented? It was this question which the great
sociologist Emile Durkheim attempted to answer in his book *The
Elementary Forms of Religious Life,* published in 1915. Taking

his cue from the widespread evidence of totemism, Durkheim drew attention to the essentially social character of religious expression. Durkheim noted that the totem is at one and the same time the representation of deity and the emblem of the society or tribal group. From this his conclusion seemed inevitable: "So if it is at once the symbol of the god and of society, is that not because the god and the society are only one?"[11] This identification Durkheim held to be not a reduction of religion but an attestation to its true and abiding significance. Thus at the beginning of his work he summarized his position as follows:

> "The general conclusion of the book which the reader has before him is that religion is something eminently social. Religious representations are collective representations which express collective realities . . ."[12]

These "collective realities," Durkheim maintained, were expressive of the social reality by which the individual transcended the limitations of particularity and was enabled to participate in a higher intellectual and moral order. This genuinely transcendent character of society, he maintained, was what legitimately excited the sentiment of religious awe.

Durkheim's view that religion is the expression of an awareness of social reality may be a mistake owing to the over emphasis upon totemism in Durkheim's research.[13] Nevertheless, it contains an important insight in which there is greater truth than in Whitehead's aphorism that "religion is what the individual does with his own solitariness."[14] For while the social and the religious are not as coterminous as Durkheim would have them to be, it is nevertheless the case that the religious imagination does function to create and sustain a community.

In the preceding chapter we noted how society is generally sustained by images and symbols and we took that occasion to emphasize that imagination is not to be understood as the function of the individual alone. This "collective consciousness," Jung's postulate of the "collective unconscious" and the peculiar character of great art to be at once subjective and universal, all attest to the social character of human imagination. This is no less so when we come to speak of the religious imagination, and it is to Durkheim's credit that he has drawn attention so strongly to this characteristic of religion. Its significance for theological method will become increasingly clear as we proceed.

Durkheim had noted and indeed insisted upon the distinction between the sacred and the profane but had made no great use of it.[15] The task of fully elaborating and systematically employing this distinction fell to the two most influential students of the phenomenology of religion of our century, Gerardus van der Leeuw[16] and Mircea Eliade. It is to the latter of these that we turn to complete our investigation of the nature of religion.

First, we may note that what unites these two students of religion is a common method—that of phenomenology. The attempt to reduce religion to something else as its origin is gone, as are attempts to secure its ground in divine agency. The concern, as in this essay, is to attempt to elucidate the structures exhibited by the phenomena, the appearances, of religion. This procedure serves to protect the phenomena by restraining the investigator's propensity to place them on the procrustean bed of a conceptual scheme derived from elsewhere. The application of this method has resulted in a revolution in our understanding of religion.

Thus viewed, religion manifests itself as the representation of and response to the manifestation of the sacred in the midst of the profane. "In fact, this paradoxical coming-together of sacred and profane, being and non-being, absolute and relative, the eternal and the becoming, is what every hierophany (manifestation of the sacred), even the most elementary, reveals."[17] The sacred as thus represented is that which is most fully real; powerful-originative and sustaining of that which is. Religious imagination therefore may be characterized as the imaginative representation of the presence of this power or reality in the midst of human existence in the world.

The sacred thus represented is not an object of reflection or worship in and of itself but precisely at the point of its intersection and conjunction with the human world. It is thus represented as that which from the beginning grounds and founds that world and secures it from the threatening chaos of disorder and "non-being." Myth serves to relate by narrative the world of human experience to the generative power from which it springs and to which it owes its existence.

The representation of the manifestation of the sacred in myth and symbol is one which tends to gather together the various dimensions and regions of human experience and imagination and to knit them together by virtue of the common and binding thread of the sacred. The multiple levels of significance therefore in a religious symbol ". . . all converge towards a common aim: to abolish the limits of the 'fragment' man is within society and the cosmos, and by means of making clear his deepest identity and his social status, and making him one with the rhythms of nature—integrating him into a larger unity: society, the universe."[18] Thus, "thanks chiefly to his symbols, the *real existence* of primitive man was not the broken and alienated existence lived by civilized man today."[19]

At its core then religion is the representation by rite, myth, and symbol of the presence of that sacred power by virtue of which all regions and dimensions of human existence are knit together in a fabric of interwoven significance and value. This is why it is tempting to locate the nature of religion in some one of these regions, individual, social, economic, natural, or cosmic. In the mythic universe of meaning each of them is so tied to the others that it may seem to be the key to the whole. That, however, to which the religious imagination points as the special source of this unity is not one of these regions but the holy or sacred itself constituting no independent region of experience alone but imbuing each and all with its sustaining power.

We have said that imagination is the symbolic transformation of the given. In the case of the religious imagination that "given" is the presence and power of the sacred in the midst of the profane. This in itself leads us to suggest that the "given" for religious imagination is the "giving" of itself of the sacred. At the core of religion is grace—the transfiguration of the sheer givenness of reality into the granted, gifted, and in that sense truly given, character of reality. Humanity ekes out existence for the most part in the poverty of being amidst a scarcity of means and abilities wherewith to survive. Into this kingdom of necessity there appears in whatever guise and from whatever source an excess of being, power, value, and significance. This sheer overflow of being creates a space of abundance and therefore of freedom which, however it may be hedged in and protected by custom, taboo, and rite, is thereby also made available to inaugurate, if only for the dura-

tion of the sacred dance or story, the kingdom of freedom. This
is the justification for van der Leeuw's claim that all religions
without exception are religions of salvation.[20]

THE RELIGIOUS SYMBOL

We must now look somewhat more carefully at the character
of religious images. Religious language, as Feuerbach has noted, is
poetic language in distinction to the language of science which is or
seeks to be literal. Of course, no language is a sheerly literal and
direct transcription of reality—it is always a patterning and transformation of that reality. The essay by Owen Barfield entitled
Saving the Appearances is subtitled "A Study of Idolatry" because
it documents the way in which in the modern period we have
allowed ourselves to be seduced into believing that our language
is just such a literal transcription, thereby substituting the image
for the real. This peculiarly modern heresy infects not only some
forms of scientific thought but has also managed to penetrate into
the religious sphere engendering the peculiar modern heresies of
fundamentalism and biblical literalism.

In religious language, however, we have a product of imagination
which is quite recalcitrant to this sort of confusion. In fact, one
of the reasons that religious language gave so much trouble to the
analytical philosophy of the earlier part of this century was because
of its consistent erosion of the logic of univocity The most extreme forms of this logical positivism maintained that if the language in which religion found its most typical expression did not
"mean" in the same way as assertions such as, "the cup is on the
table," or "two plus two equal four" mean, then that language
must be sheer nonsense or "merely emotive." This linguistic
analysis did produce a considerable advance in clarity with respect
to many philosophic issues. When the dust had settled and it
became clear that philosophers' frowns and incantations such as
"meaningless" or "emotive" did not drive out all other forms of
language, it was increasingly realized that there are indeed multiple
ways in which words and sentences have meaning—that the association of religion with poetry might not be simply disparaging (to
either) but might contain a clue as to the structure of meaning
previously overlooked.

Much work remains to be done in clarifying the way in which
highly symbolic language structures like poetry and myth function

to convey meaning, but we have at least learned that they do not convey meaning in the way in which "empirical-scientific" or mathematic language structures have been thought to do. The key to an understanding of the way in which religious language function has been sought and to an extent found in its "symbolic" character. We must therefore pay some attention to the character of the religious symbol.

It is Paul Tillich who among recent theologians has most clearly appreciated the character of the religious symbol, and it is therefore appropriate that we should first turn to him for an understanding of its character. In the *Dynamics of Faith* he points to general characteristics of symbols which may be paraphrased as follows:[21]

1. they point beyond themselves
2. they participate in that to which they point
3. they open up dimensions of reality external to ourselves which are otherwise inaccessible
4. they open up commensurate dimensions of our internal reality equally inaccessible
5. they cannot be intentionally produced
6. they grow and die corresponding to their ability or inability to give expression to and mediate to a human community the reality to which they point.

The first thing to be noted here is that a symbol is not simply an arbitrary label which merely serves conveniently to denote and classify some object. Much of our language does seem to function in that way. But symbols, insofar as they function authentically, mediate, convey, make present and effective that to which they also point. Peoples, we are told, who are not yet caught up in the wave of what we are pleased to call civilization, still live within a linguistic world which is very much a symbolic one in this regard. The very name invokes the reality named. There is a certain inconvenience in this to be sure. For example, if the uttering of the word "fire" conjured up in our minds so vivid an impression of raging conflagration as to make it difficult or impossible to restrain our panic, it would make a sober discussion of fire prevention difficult indeed. But there is the opposite difficulty that when words become so stripped of the reality to which they refer, apparently sane conversations become possible regarding mega-deaths and body-counts, which proceed with less heat than a discussion of batting averages. The irreplaceable function of the symbol is that of truly mediating, thereby making it possible for us actually to participate in the reality to which it points. This is precisely why it is ludicrous to think of creating new symbols and myths. For the power of mediating reality cannot be arbitrarily conjured or attached. It is a power which a symbol has because it resonates with the experience and history which it has also in part created.

Because of this mediating power the symbol simultaneously evokes and invokes. That is, it evokes the reality of our existence at the same time that it invokes that reality within which we dwell. It is sometimes said, though I think incorrectly, that the symbol abolishes the subject-object distinction. That would not be mediation or participation but confusion. Instead the symbol brings to awareness simultaneously interior and exterior, subjective and objective, by establishing between them a mutuality of meaning. The crucial point, however, is that this reality, interior or exterior, is present only as mediated by the symbol. Without the symbol the reality of my own existence, or of the world within which I live, falls away from awareness. My connectedness to myself and to reality is severed. I am cast adrift to divert my attention, as long as I am able, from the exterior abyss and the internal void. Somewhat in this vein, Nathan Scott has declared that the literature of our period reflects this trauma. "The trauma that has been suffered is the trauma that is inflicted upon the imagination when it appears that both God and man are dead."[22]

This returns us to the theme of the religious symbol. It is the religious symbol which relates the various regions of an otherwise fragmented experience to one another by virtue of the presence of that which is their ground, that is, the sacred. But the religious symbol represents the reality of the sacred not in itself but in its relation to some one or several such regions. The independent being of God is a preoccupation of philosophy, not religion. Religion only has interest in the presence and acting of the sacred. Thus, as Tillich points out: "Religious symbols are double-edged. They are directed toward the infinite which they symbolize and the finite through which they symbolize it."[23] This is so because the sacred (or infinite as Tillich here calls it) is known to religion only in conjunction with the profane reality into which it comes in conjunction in the hierophany or manifestation. Now this means that religious expression cannot be other than symbolic. It is not reducible to language about the world, to language about existence, or to language about the "being" of God (to use the language of the philosophical tradition). It is in this respect necessarily pluri-significative, multi-referential, or polysemous. To replace this mani-fold of meaning with some one level of meaning is to utterly divest it of its capacity for mediation. There is, as Tillich rightly asserts, "no substitute for the use of symbols and myths: they are the language of faith."[24]

This brings us then to the question of "demythologizing." It was David Friedrich Strauss who first suggested a program of interpreting the four gospels as mythic.[25] The mythic character of these gospels, reaching a culmination in the Gospel of John, he regarded as their truth. He was a student of Hegel and so was persuaded that the mythic expressions of a people are representa-tive of their deepest but imperfectly understood insights. Myth is the coming to expression of Absolute Spirit in human consciousness and as such is of fundamental importance. But this expression is defective, it has not yet been appropriated by the understanding. It is the task of philosophy to give final and adequate expression to that which is imperfectly expressed in the myth.

Like Strauss, Bultmann a century later was persuaded that there is much that is mythic in the New Testament, that it was an expression of truth but he also, like Strauss, maintained that it was a defective mode of expression. It was the mythic form of expres-sion, he was persuaded, that tended to make the interior meaning recede from our grasp. Conservatives battled with skeptics over the husks and failed to see the truth within. Bultmann was deter-mined that the truth of the Christian faith should be freed from the "false scandal" of an outmoded and defective mode of expression. The project of liberation upon which he embarked he called "demythologization." When the conservatives complained that he was putting the edifice of faith to the torch, he replied in effect that he would watch it burn cheerfully, for what was consumed was the husk (Jesus according to the flesh, as he said) and the true would abide unscathed but purified.[26]

Now there is much to be said for Bultmann's project, and espe-cially for the devotion to truth, above all, by which it was carried through. He is clearly without peer in this century among New Testament scholars, and his project of demythologization has enlivened and enriched the study of the New Testament. In retro-

spect, however, it must be said that the proposal for demythologizing was not formulated with the precision that has subsequently
become necessary. For it failed to take into sufficient account the
sense in which religious language is *necessarily* symbolic and mythical. Bultmann was right in supposing that much unnecessary
difficulty was caused by the clash between an ancient and a modern
world view. Bultmann was not prepared, some of his critics to the
contrary notwithstanding, simply to capitulate to a modern world
view. His retention of the kerygmatic center of faith is sufficient
proof of that. But he was persuaded that the mythic terminology
could be replaced by an existential anthropology without losing the
essential of faith and with the gain of insight into the meaning of
the texts, or at least one level of that meaning. In this he was
largely right. The gain in understanding was, however, purchased
at the price of discounting the actual character of the mythic.
What set out to be an interpretation always remained in danger of
becoming a reduction.[27] Bultmann's critics on the left like Ogden
and Buri complained that he did not go far enough with his project
and that he was inconsistent in not doing so. They were insisting
on the philosophic reduction which Bultmann refused.[28] The
demand for this further reduction might have received a more
cogent response if it had been possible more accurately to characterize the task of interpreting mythic language than was possible
given the project of "demythologizing."

Subsequently Paul Ricoeur has introduced a very useful distinction between what he calls the explanatory and the exploratory
character of mythic language.[29] The former is that tendency of
mythical language to assume the status of a scientific or pseudo-
scientific description and explanation of reality. It is this which
accounts for that collision between an ancient (presumably mythic)
and contemporary world view in which the former is bound to lose
to the latter. By contrast, the exploratory character of mythic
language is what we have been calling its mediating and symbolic
character—that is, its way of relating human life to the sacred,
thus permeating existence and world with a structure of significance. It is this latter which is neither reducible nor replaceable.
Bultmann was forever in danger of allegorizing the mythic language
—of substituting for it the more direct rendering of an existential
anthropology. But as Ricoeur notes, mythic language "is not
reducible to any translation in cipher to a clear language."[30] It is

this very irreducibility of the mythic that makes it perennially provocative of reflection. It both grounds and engenders that reflection and without it reflection is liable to become lifeless and arid. The symbol, Ricoeur says, gives rise to thought.[31] That, to anticipate, is the guiding thread of this essay.

THE MODES OF THE RELIGIOUS IMAGINATION

Up to now in this chapter we have used the terms myth and symbol interchangeably to designate the results of religious imagination. While this procedure can and will be justified, it is necessary to discriminate some of the chief modes through which the religious imagination comes to expression. This may give some idea of the richness and diversity of the phenomena which are included under the broad heading of the religious imagination.

Since in the preceding chapter we had occasion to look at the phenomena of dreams in relation to the unconscious, the first mode of religious imagination to which we will give our attention is that of the vision. The vision is probably the least popular mode of the religious imagination. It is the one most subject to the charge of being subjective in the sense of being private in significance. It is the one most susceptible to the classic put down: "it was probably something you ate." Nevertheless the vision is a significant mode of religious imagination and some attention must be given to it.

By a "vision" in this context we mean the emergence either in dream, trance, or ecstasy, of a pattern of images, words, or dream-like dramas which are experienced then, and upon later reflection, as having revelatory significance. Thus vision in this context is used also to include what are sometimes called auditions as, for example, in the celebrated case of Joan of Arc. It should also be noted that some vision-like phenomena resist expression in word or image as in the case of the mystics' beatific vision. This may be understood as the report of a state of consciousness in which the imagination properly does not come into play and if so it falls outside our present consideration.

The vision in any event is experienced as coming from outside the person—that is, as being independent of volition and as disclosing some aspect of ultimate reality. The vision may be limited in its significance to the individual, but more usually it is understood to have import for an entire community, or perhaps for the history of humanity. Although it is not in keeping with at least

some customary usage, I believe that it is appropriate to restrict
the category of religious vision to those visions whose significance
is not restricted to the individual, but rather pertains to an entire
religious community (or a significant segment of it) and is understood by that community as of revelatory significance. This at any
rate is the more important class of visions from the standpoint of a
phenomenology of the religious imagination. It is this social significance of the religious vision which distinguishes it, though it
does not clearly separate it, from those dreams and visions which
on account of their idiosyncratic character have become the special
province of psychiatry and psychoanalysis. This is not to deny the
significance of the latter for a phenomenology of religion but only
to distinguish the former as of greater significance—for religion, as
Durkheim has argued, is at least preeminently social.

Despite what Jung characterizes as the reluctance at least of
Protestant theologians to understand the dream or dream-like
phenomena as the *vox dei*,[32] it is clear that visions have a great
significance in the Judeo-Christian tradition as well as functioning
importantly in many "primitive" religious communities. A number
of such visions figure in biblical literature: Isaiah's vision in the
temple, Ezekiel's visions, the vision on the Mount of Transfiguration, etc. Recently Wolfhart Pannenberg has suggested the importance of this category of vision for an understanding of the
resurrection appearances.[33]

A second general mode of the religious imagination is the symbol.
In its narrowest sense the symbol is a fundamentally non-verbal
representation of the conjunction of the sacred and the profane.
Here some prominent feature of the circumambient world represents and mediates the hierophany (a blasted tree, Mt. Sinai, a
sacred animal), or an object specially crafted for this purpose (a
totem, crucifix, the golden calf) may also serve this function.

When we think of a symbol in this sense we get a better appreciation for what is meant by speaking of the symbolic function in
a more generalized sense. For example, the totem of a particular
group may be the representation of a fox. This representation,
however, does not primarily designate a particular fox or foxes in
general. It also designates the group—its identity as a community
together with all the mores and taboos which regulate its life.
Moreover, it establishes the identity of that group within its world
—in relation to nature and other groups. Finally, it signifies that

power from which the group emerges and by which it is sustained —that is, the sacred. All this it does at the same time. All of these threads of significance are drawn together in the symbol and made present by it as a unity. "Symbol" means to draw or throw together. It is, I think, misleading to speak of something as a "symbol of the sacred," for the religious symbol unites the sacred with existence and the world and represents not the sacred as such but this coming together which is the work of the sacred. To say then that religious language is symbolic draws attention to its *pluri*-signative character.

A third general mode of the religious imagination is the myth. Much debate is possible about whether symbols are concentrated myths (Eliade) or, as Ricoeur seems to suggest, myths are expositions or a linking together of symbols. It does not seem to be necessary to give a final answer to this question. They are usually quite distinct forms of the religious imagination. Although they do interpenetrate or influence one another, they are, I maintain, distinct modalities of the religious imagination which normally reinforce one another.

While the symbol, narrowly understood, is primarily non-verbal, the myth is fundamentally verbal. It is a narration which conveys the meaning of human existence in relation to its destiny or origin, or the destiny or origin of the social group, nature, or cosmos of which it is a part, as these are grounded and penetrated by the sacred.

The myth serves as a paradigm or model for the orientation of understanding, behavior, and attitude. As we have seen, the myth does not stand as a competitor to scientific explanation or historical fact, but rather serves to direct and interpret human existence and experience in the light of the meaning imparted by confrontation with the sacred. The myth is not to be understood as a literal statement referring to some particular fact, nor is it to be understood in contrast to fact as though it always entails make believe. The raw material of the myth may be fact or fancy but its purpose is not to add yet another fact to our squirrels' nest of facts stored against some winter of the mind, nor to create an entertaining fantasy to titillate aesthetic delight. The intention of myth is to narrate the fundamental structure of human being in the world. By the concreteness of its imagery, the universality of its intention, its narrative or story form, the myth evokes the identifi-

cation and participation of those for whom it functions as revelatory. Insofar as it is myth rather than pseudo-science or legend,
it is not disinterested. Furthermore, it is subjective in the sense
of making a claim upon its hearers to understand their existence
and world from the perspective of the myth.

We may note in this connection that the myth does not in the first
instance require or seek to be interpreted. It is, as Ricoeur has
noted, itself an interpretation.[34] It itself serves as the hermeneutical key to unlock the meaning of existence and world. Insofar
as it functions religiously it is its own interpretation. The interpreter who sets out to understand the myth must first consent to
being interpreted by the myth (at least provisionally), or the
meaning of the myth has been lost altogether. The special application of this insight to the field of New Testament interpretation
characterizes what has been called the new hermeneutic.[35] In any
case, the myth is not a code or allegory to be deciphered. Rather it
purports to be in some sense itself the decipherment of reality.

A fourth mode of the religious imagination is that of ritual. The
form of the ritual is public dramatic action usually involving some
combination of dance, chant, sacrifice, or sacrament.

In the ritual one of the central features of religious imagination
comes directly to the forefront—namely, its essential sociality. The
ritual is a group enactment of and participation in the presence of
the sacred. As both Durkheim and Malinowski have noted, it is
characteristically public.

The ritual is a fundamental mode of the religious imagination and
yet it is probably the one form (next to vision) least apppreciated
by our Protestant-dominated sensibility. We tend to distrust it,
either because it is a rigid routine (thus eliminating spontaneity),
or because it relies upon meaningless actions which seem to be
occult or magical. Both of these notions about ritual are, however,
mistaken. Ritual is the opposite of routine in its aim to express
and mediate the extraordinary. It is rigid only in the sense of being
patterned activity, but this patterning is precisely what makes possible the expressive participation of the public.[36] Moreover, it is
the intent of ritual to disclose rather than to obscure the dimension
of ultimate reality to which it points. It resists the literal and
intellectual reduction which is so generally the norm for mainline
Protestant groups in this country. Precisely in the way in which
it directs attention away from itself and involves the actual physical

participation of the group, the ritual has the capacity to elude reduction to literal statement. Unfortunately, much liturgical renewal
in Protestantism and Catholicism has moved in the opposite direction, thereby further literalizing and banalizing ritual to the point
of religious insignificance.

A fifth mode of religious imagination of less general importance
than the others is that of apocalyptic. It is included here because
of its importance for an understanding of the Christian imagination
to be considered subsequently. Like myth, apocalyptic is verbal
(often written) yet it is cast in the form of a vision. Unlike the
myth whose typical reference is to the time of origin, the reference
of apocalyptic is to the absolute future. Although it is stylized as a
vision it tends to be anonymous (or pseudonymous) and generally
quite elaborate in contrast to the relatively simple character of the
vision.

Apocalyptic seems, in general, to be restricted to expressions of
the religious imagination deriving from the Near East (Zorastrian-
ism, Judaism, Christianity, and Islam) although it is also found
among populations which seem to have been influenced at least
partly by Christian, or post-Christian religious influences (Mormon-
ism and Jehovah's Witnesses, for example). Thus it finds expression among colonialized peoples in America (Ghost Dance, Peyote
Cult), Africa (Kitower), and Polynesia (Cargo Cults).[37]

Despite the fact that it has long been disparaged in theology
and philosophy, apocalyptic has begun to receive new attention as it
becomes clear that it is crucial for an understanding of the eschatological character of the Christian mythos as well as shedding important insight on the relationship of faith to political (especially
revolutionary) involvement. It does seem too that this increased
interest in apocalyptic cannot fail to sharpen the awareness of the
fundamental role played by imagination in the life of religion and
particularly that of Christianity. If that is so it cannot help but be
of benefit both to the life of faith and to the liveliness of theology.

Having separated these various modes of the religious imagination, it is necessary to emphasize that in any religious tradition in
which they are to be found, they tend to be assimilated to one
another to constitute a unified but kaleidoscopically ramifying symbolic structure. In this essay that total structure is referred to as
a mythos. Of course, that in part reflects the bias of a Christian
or perhaps Protestant perspective upon religion. But though it

does suggest the primacy of the mythic (and thereby narrative) mode of religious imagination, it may also usefully serve to designate a complex composed of many elements, some of which are mythic and others of which are myth-like in structure and intention if not in form.

THE FUNCTIONS OF THE RELIGIOUS IMAGINATION

We must now examine the way in which the mythos functions to mediate and represent the sacred. Here I will identify four ways of functioning which, while they are generally characteristic of the religious imagination, are also of direct importance for an understanding of the Christian mythos. *The functions of the mythos are those of representation, orientation, communication, and transformation.*

The mythos represents the relation of existence and world to the sacred. It is important to remember that this representation is first of all a transfiguration rather than a transcription of the reality thus represented. Imagination generally, whether in perception, dream, or myth, is not a mere transmitter of data—it is fundamentally creative and active in the shaping, the "figuration," of that which it represents. But this is not to say that the products of the imagination generally, or of religious imagination specifically, are instances of *creatio ex nihilo*. In perception we are confident in supposing that what is thus transfigured itself constitutes a limit to the creativity or activity of image formation. Similarly, we have learned to think of the dream as representative of the unconscious intentions and dynamics which, though they are transfigured in the dream symbols, are nevertheless themselves present in those symbols. Likewise in the case of the religious imagination we speak of the sacred as that which in its relation to the profane is thus represented. The reality of the sacred, like that of the unconscious or the circumambient world, is one to which we have no direct immediate access. Rather, access is mediated by the image alone which contributes its creative act in the formulation of that image by which it represents the sacred to us.

Thus the representation supplied by the mythos cannot be simply and directly checked against the reality it purports to represent. It may be compared with some other range of symbols, mythic or otherwise, but finally verification springs from the way in which the person or community recognizes the representation. Then occurs what Ian Ramsey calls a disclosure situation in which "the penny drops."[38] This is the ground, indeed the only possible ground, for speaking of the authority of the mythos. This can never be an authority imposed or guaranteed from outside, but occurs when one recognizes oneself and one's world as represented by the mythos. This, I think, is what some theologians mean when they speak of the kerygma being self-authenticating. This is what some Christian groups mean by conversion when they speak of it as "coming under conviction of sin"—that is, recognizing one's plight as that to which the mythos speaks.

The mythos in representing existence in relation to the sacred also orients that existence in relation to the multiple dimensions and horizons of its reality. Existence is positional with respect to birth and death, love and hate, individual and society, nature and history, cosmos and life. When referring to the religious symbol (and thus by extension, all elements of a mythos) we noted that in it the several regions of reality are drawn together and concentrated at the point of the meeting of the sacred and profane.

It is because of this multi-dimensionality intrinsic to the mythos that it functions to orient life in relation to these dimensions—introducing a pattern of significance which ramifies endlessly yet is ordered by the unifying and engendering power of the sacred which it mediates.

Thus the mythos by patterning these regions of reality opens them to experience, granting them to experience and participation. This orienting and patterning function may seem at first to be an inhibiting of free access to these dimensions of experience, an over-structuring of reality. But unstructured, unpatterned reality is, as William James suggested, "a blooming buzzing confusion." It is more than that, however—it is an alien abyss. Patterning is the very heart of significance or meaning, and the absolutely unpatterned is the absolutely meaningless, indeed, the devourer of meaning and thus of being. Of course, we are all aware of the presence of patterns and structures which have lost their meaning and manifest only the dead hand of the past upon the throat of life. We are also aware of those whose mythos or perhaps world-view serves to truncate experience or close it off from some dimension of reality. But the authentic function of a mythos is not to impose patterns that don't

fit or to limit meaningful participation in reality. Instead it functions to orient life to all the dimensions of reality, thus opening
them for full and meaningful participation.

The mythos by its public and social nature functions to communicate existence and thus to establish and sustain community.
Indeed the mythos is both the product and the creator of a community of faith. It is the product of that community in that it is
the result of the encounter of that community with the sacred in
nature and history. But it also creates that community in that, by
naming and structuring the social reality, it makes the experience
of and participation in it possible.

Moreover, the mythos constitutes for a religious community the
circulatory system through which life communicates with life.
Through shared images and language which identify and make
mutual the meanings by which the existence of persons is sustained,
a vehicle for intimacy is provided. In the shared language of the
mythos one shares in the fundamental structure of meaning which
sustains the life of the other. One of the primary causes of that
sense of radical separation which characterizes so much contemporary culture is the loss or trivialization of such a system of shared
meanings; much of the attraction of arcane religious movements,
whether imported from other times and cultures or produced by
charismatic and fundamentalist versions of Christianity, is the way
in which they serve to overcome the isolation caused by the trivialization of symbols.

Finally, the mythos functions to transform behavior and perception to accord with its representation of reality. In stable religious
communities this process of transformation is an organic one moving the person easily into the altered perceptions and behavior
complementary to age and status, as in the rites of passage. But
in other societies this transformational character is more pro-
nounced and sometimes drastic. The conversion experience which
is such a regular feature of Christian tradition is one of the clearest
examples. Here it is a case of moving from one mythos to
another, or of moving from a non-mythic to a religious perspective,
or of moving from a nominally to an actually religious framework
of meaning. In these more dramatic expressions of the transformational function, it is clear that the mythos not only represents
existence but places upon that existence a claim to interpret it in

such a way as to alter everything. When Jesus is reported to have commanded the leaving of family and work we have an example of how totally the alteration of mythos entails the alteration of relationship to all dimensions of one's experience.

We have already noted the way in which imagination generally entails a transformation of its given into symbol. In speaking now of the transformative function of a mythos we see how the mythos transforms the awareness and thus the behavior of the subject and of the community. This sense of transformation is thus related to the more general one but has a reflexive (changing perception) and an imperative (changing behavior) character.

The reason for emphasizing this function independently is to direct attention to the fact that a mythos is not simply a species of world view or a perspective from which one looks. These images fail to convey the intimate connection between seeing and doing —or, in terms more directly related to the Judeo-Christian tradition, hearing and doing. The mythos is not simply an indicative but also and fundamentally an imperative. However we may have to define the truth of a mythos, it is always a truth that one *does* rather than a truth one may simply acknowledge. This is of importance for our subsequent discussion of theological method since it supports the view of Karl Barth that theology and ethics can only by a fatal misunderstanding be construed as two separate disciplines.

I have discriminated four functions of the mythos. Clearly they are intimately interrelated in such a way that one is invariably accompanied by the other three. By separating them in this way, however, it should have become apparent that what is usually and properly summarized as the interpretive or mediative function of symbolic or mythic language is not a simple but a quite complex and far reaching thing indeed. In summary then *the religious imagination through the mythos serves to express and make effective the presence of the sacred in such a way as to represent, orient, communicate, and transform existence in the world.*

NOTES

1. Friedrich Schleiermacher, *The Christian Faith*, trans. H. R. Mackintosh and J. S. Stewart (New York: Harper & Row, 1963), I, pp. 31 ff.

2. Paul Tillich, *Christianity and the Encounter with the World Religions* (New York: Columbia University Press, 1963).

3. E. B. Tyler, *Primitive Culture* (2 vols.; London: Murray, 1873).

4. Sigmund Freud, *The Future of an Illusion*, trans. James Strachey (New York: Doubleday-Anchor, 1964).

5. Karl Barth, *Protestant Theology in the Nineteenth Century* (Valley Forge; Judson Press, 1973), pp. 534 ff.

6. Ludwig Feuerbach, *Lectures on the Essence of Religion*, trans. Ralph Manheim (New York: Harper and Row, 1967), p. 181.

7. *Ibid.*, p. 178.

8. *Ibid.*, p. 180.

9. *Ibid.*

10. Cf. Karl Barth, *Evangelical Theology* (New York: Holt, Rinehart & Winston, 1963), pp. 30–31.

11. Emile Durkheim, *The Elementary Forms of the Religious Life*, trans. J. W. Swain (New York: Macmillan, 1915).

12. *Ibid.*, p. 10.

13. Cf. Bronislaw Malinowski, *Magic, Science and Religion.* (Garden City, New York: Doubleday-Anchor, 1954), pp. 55 ff.

14. A. N. Whitehead, *Religion in the Making* (Cleveland: Meridian Books, 1960), p. 16.

15. Malinowski, *op. cit.*, p. 58.

16. The most important work of Gerardus van der Leeuw is *Religion in Essence and Manifestation,* trans. J. E. Turner (2 vols.; New York: Harper & Row, 1963). For a description of the phenomenological method cf. *Ibid.,* II, pp. 671–678. Consideration of various methodologies for the discipline may be found in *The History of Religion: Essays in Methodology,* ed. Mircea Eliade and Joseph Kitagawa (Chicago: University of Chicago Press, 1959).

17. Mircea Eliade, *Patterns in Comparative Religion*, trans. Rosemary Sheed (New York: Sheed and Ward, 1958), p. 29.

18. *Ibid.*, p. 451.

19. *Ibid.*, p. 456.

20. Van der Leeuw, *op. cit., p. 682.*

21. Paul Tillich, *Dynamics of Faith* (New York: Harper Torchbooks, 1958), pp. 41–43.

22. Nathan Scott, "The Broken Center: The Crisis of Values in Modern Literature," *Symbolism in Religion and Literature,* ed. Rollo May (New York: George Brazillier, 1960), p. 196.

23. Paul Tillich, *Systematic Theology*, I, p. 240.

24. Paul Tillich, *Dynamics of Faith*, p. 51.

25. David Friedrich Strauss, *The Life of Jesus Critically Examined,* trans. George Eliot (Philadelphia: Fortress Press, 1972), pp. 39–92.

26. Rudolph Bultmann, "On the Question of Christology," *Faith and Understanding,* I, trans. L. R. Smith. (New York: Harper and Row, 1969), pp. 131–132.

27. See Bonhoeffer's critique of Bultmann in *Letters and Papers,* enlarged edition, ed. Eberhard Bethge (New York: The Macmillan Company, 1972), p. 285.

28. For Schubert Ogden's critique see his *Christ Without Myth.* (New York: Harper & Row, 1967). For Buri's position cf. Fritz Buri, "Entmythologisierung oder Entkerygmatisierung der Theologie," *Kerygma und Mythos,* ed. H.-W. Bartsch. (Hamburg: Harbert Reich, 1952), II, pp. 85–101.

29. Paul Ricoeur, *The Symbolism of Evil*, p. 5.

30. *Ibid.*, p. 163.
31. *Ibid.*, p. 348.
32. C. G. Jung, *Man and His Symbols,* p. 93.
33. Wolfhart Pannenberg, *Jesus: God and Man*, trans. Lewis L. Wilkins and Duane A. Priebe (Philadelphia: The Westminster Press, 1968), pp. 74 ff.
34. Ricoeur, *op. cit.*, p. 237.
35. For an early discussion of this issue cf. James M. Robinson and John B. Cobb (eds.), *The New Hermeneutic* (New York: Harper and Row, 1964).
36. Suzanne Langer, *op. cit.*, pp. 127–148.
37. Vittorio Lanternari, *Religions of the Oppressed*, trans. Lisa Sergio New York: Mentor, 1965).
38. Ian T. Ramsey, *Religious Language* (New York: Macmillan, 1963).

Chapter 5

The Christian Mythos

In this chapter we turn to a direct confrontation with the Christian mythos. Our previous discussion of the character of symbols and of a religious mythos will guide our discussion here, serving as a framework for an understanding of the character of the Christian mythos.

THE RELIGIOUS CHARACTER OF CHRISTIANITY

Before proceeding to a characterization of that mythos it is necessary to take account of some of the objections which may arise here. The objections I will attempt to meet are: 1) the kerygma is not a myth; 2) Christianity is not a religion; 3) if Christianity is a religion it can be of no concern for secular experience.

The first objection may be based upon contrasting a) history and myth or b) revelation and myth. I have no desire to deny either the historical or the revelatory character of the Christian story by calling it a product of the imagination—specifically a mythos. Later on in this chapter some attention will be given to the question of historicity and a full chapter will be devoted to it in Part II. At this point it will be enough to say that the historical base of the Christian mythos has been transfigured into the representation of the presence of the sacred in our world. It is no less history but it is a particular kind of history—it is presented as the history of salvation.[1] Nor does mythos stand in contrast to revelation although the question of revelation is postponed by our loosely phenomenological approach until the end of this essay. It can only be reaffirmed here that this approach is not intended to be prejudicial to the question of the truth which is given expression in the images and narratives of Christian faith. However one may formulate a doctrine of revelation, it is necessary to formulate it in such a way as to say that revelation occurs and comes to expression through human words and symbols which attempt to convey that which has been "seen and heard." What is implicitly being denied here is a doctrine of literal inspiration which entails the absolute suppression of human imagination and intelligence in the transmission of or witness to that revelation.

The second objection is somewhat more serious since it seems to represent an important insight into the theology of, among others, Barth and Bonhoeffer. Barth's objection[2] may be represented as follows: religion is the attempt of human beings to reach toward God; Christian faith is the account of God's reaching toward human beings. The first is human aspiration; the second, divine condescension. Barth is attempting here to cut the Gordian knot of relativism introduced into theology by the nineteenth century study of religion. It should be noted, however, that his objection is not to the disciplines of comparative religions but to what he construes to be a corruption of Christian faith. It is the religion in Christendom against which he is striking. I am in entire accord with the distinction which Barth makes between one's attempt to rescue oneself from the world and the assertion that one has been liberated by another. That distinction is fundamental and is indeed the distinction of law and gospel. It is not, however, a distinction which is accurately or helpfully expressed as one between religion and faith. I have used the term religion to refer to the response to the sacred. To assert that Christianity is a religion in that sense in no way *need* conflict with the theological judgment that Barth was rendering.

The objection of Bonhoeffer is somewhat different although he was influenced by Barth and sought to sharpen Barth's objection. Bonhoeffer's position, scattered in the fragments of his prison writings, has been often misconstrued. Bonhoeffer sought to deny that Christianity has to do with the private sector of piety secluded from the world. The two words with which Bonhoeffer principally associates religion are "inwardness" and metaphysics."[3] Both are a flight from the actual reality of our world and it is with this actual world that Christian faith has to do. Bonhoeffer is sometimes thought of as a secular theologian in the reductionist mode. Such interpretations are in fundamental error as is shown by Bonhoeffer's own disclaimer of any intention to abridge or reduce the Christian faith—something which he could still accuse Bultmann of doing in the latter's project of demythologizing.[4] Bonhoeffer's objection then is made in the name of the fundamental worldliness of Christian faith. It is this very worldliness, and one may even say secularity, that I wish to stress by maintaining that Christianity *is* a religion, and this is made clear by what I have stressed about the functions of the mythos.[5] This is a convenient place to note that despite all appearances to the contrary, I believe my description of theology to be in essential though not explicit continuity with fundamental insights of both Barth and Bonhoeffer. There is no space in an essay of this scope and intent to demonstrate the continuities, but it may be helpful to the reader to assert at least that they exist.

The objection that Christianity is not a religion, or at least that it should transcend the phase of religion in the history of human development, gained some of its support from an attempt to come to terms with the increasing secularization of our culture. It was perhaps felt by some (though I think Barth and Bonhoeffer were not among them) that the development of secularization was irreversible, and that therefore one had best accommodate oneself to it. What used to be called modern secular man had, we were told, no use for religion and so we had best cut our theology to fit.[6] Much of this may have proceeded from significant theological insight, as it does in Barth, Bonhoeffer, and Gogarten. But some of it was clearly a self-serving attempt to stay relevant (i.e., nonoffensive). We were told that people today have no interest in questions of ultimate concern and no use for symbols and myths. Having adjusted theological and ecclesiastical rhetoric to this state of affairs, we suddenly discover that the market in religion has gone bullish. Every imaginable, and some heretofore unimaginable, species of religion has found its earnest followers among a highly educated and in other matters critical generation. We have, it appears, been outflanked. Just as Paul Van Buren was asserting that all theological statements must be translated into the cash value of verifiable propositions, Thomas Altizer's books,[7] in which is to be discovered scarcely any verifiable proposition, were causing a secular generation to read theology!

Nevertheless while there is much to be applauded in the recovery of a sense for the world of myth and symbol which should follow from a renewal of interest in religion, it should not be regarded as an occasion for cheap apologetics. It may summon us to a reconsideration of the rhetoric of secularization, but it may also lead to a fresh occasion to *mis*understand the character of Christian faith so as to confuse it with charismatic, mystical, or fundamentalist religion. These all may serve the important functions ascribed to religion, as Christianity also does, but not all religion is "Christian." We shall have to give all the more careful attention to the specific and particular character of the Christian mythos—not to assert its superiority but to interpret it authentically.

THE FUNCTIONS OF THE CHRISTIAN MYTHOS

We may now turn to an attempt to give a positive definition of Christianity as a religion. The goal here is to bring forward some of the insights gained from the previous discussion of religion, and to indicate the way they are applicable to an understanding of Christian faith.

In asserting that Christianity is a religion, it is evident that this means that primary expressions and secondary elaborations of the faith are products of the imagination. This means that, whatever may be construed to be the given upon which that imagination functions, it is not immediately accessible. It is mediated to human awareness through the agency of human imagination. The claim, for example, that "God has made himself known in Jesus" does not entail direct and unmediated access to revelation. On the contrary, it entails that revelation is mediated; indeed, that apart from such mediation there is no revelation at all. But the function of mediation is not exhausted by Jesus. Indeed, we should know nothing whatever of him apart from the reports, assertions, and interpretations of his life and the significance of that life which are left to us from that community of faith which arose in response to him. The story or stories are not positivistic history but presentations of the meaning or significance of that series of events. We do not have here the transmission of facts but their symbolic transformation. Surely by this time such an assertion should cause no difficulty. It is not a denial of the viability or the veracity of such accounts. It is an assertion that the images, words, and narratives are fully and completely human. They do not drop fom heaven like a stone.

To assert that they are products of the imagination is further to assert that they do not sever the affective how from the given what. The subject and the object are not fundamentally disjoined. The stories are confessional rather than objective, just as, similarly, the images are usually sensual rather than conceptual.

This imagination is, however, religious and that means that it has reference to the sacred. This is to say that it refers to the fundamental reality of existence and world—to that power by which they are sustained and empowered to be. It is reference to that which grounds being (Tillich), which lets-be (Macquarrie), which is Holy, awesome, and overpowering (Otto). It designates that reality as "the God and Father of Jesus." The sacred thus represented is, of course, not represented in and for itself. As we have noted in the discussion of the religious imagination, the sacred is not a particular region of human experience which is represented separately from existence and world. Religious imagination has to do not with the sacred as such but with the presence of the sacred to and in the human world. Thus the Christian imagination gives expression to the presence and availability of that holy power whereby what is, is sustained in being and meaning. This too is what is involved in maintaining that Christianity is a religion. Further, it draws attention to the intention of word and symbol not merely to represent, but to make effectively present that to which they point. It is the language of invocation. It is also language which seeks to evoke that subjective reality corresponding to the presence of the sacred—namely, faith.

We have called the product of the religious imagination a mythos and have suggested that such a mythos functions in particular ways. An indication of the way in which the expressions of Christian faith function in similar ways will complete the elaboration of the way in which Christianity is to be understood as a religion.

As noted in the previous chapter, the first function of the mythos is to *represent* existence in relation to the sacred. "Mythos" in the sense in which it is being used in this essay is not a "story about the gods" which recounts supernatural exploits not fundamentally engaging the life and fate of hearer and teller. The story of Nathan and David is typical here. When Nathan tells David about the rich man stealing the poor man's sheep he may be storyteller, historian, poet, or commentator on the waywardness of human kind. When he says to David: "You are the man," he is a prophet. The religious imagination is irresistibly *ad hominem.*

Herein lies the basis for Bultmann's anthropological and existential reading of the New Testament. Cosmological and theological assertions of a mythos may and must be interpreted anthropologically.[8] The reverse, of course, is also the case—something which Bultmann also knew but did little about. This function of a mythos is particularly stressed by the kerygmatic nature of the material. It presents the hearer with a summons to a decision. Such a decision in this case springs from a recognition of one's existence as represented. It is as though one were to say: "Yes, at this or that point I recognize my own life in its concrete reality." The intention of the Christian mythos is not to obscure but to illumine existence. Insofar as it does so it has authority. It is in this sense that hearing is already faith, as the Gospel of John asserts.[9]

The mythos also functions to orient existence. It situates one within a pattern of meaning interpretive of life and death, nature and history, work and play, individual and community. We have noted how the religious symbol gathers together the multiple dimensions of reality and life thereby unifying the human world in the light of the sacred. The Christian mythos also serves this function. The Gothic cathedral, as is often noted, is an example of the bringing together of all the experiences of life under the aegis of the mythos. But it is not simply in medieval culture that this occurs. The recognition of which we have already spoken may also become an interpretation. That is, one may come to see more and more of oneself and one's world from the perspective of the mythos. Insofar as the mythos does function to orient existence it functions to open up the multiple dimensions of life to full and meaningful participation. Christian self-understanding certainly is not to be restricted to some one sector of life—the so-called religious sphere. There is no such isolated sphere.[10]

The mythos functions to communicate existence. It is important also to stress here the way in which the Christian mythos establishes community. The social character of religion has been stressed repeatedly and the Christian mythos is not an exception to this. Despite the popular refrain that Christianity (or sometimes the Judeo-Christian tradition) discovered or specially emphasized the individual, it is no less characteristic that it also emphasizes the communtiy. The word which communicates also creates community. The mythos which summons to decision is also the center of the community of faith. The community is constituted by the mythos. The mutual participation in a shared pattern of meaning makes possible the identification with and appropriate participation in the life of the other. So important is this characteristic of the Christian mythos that it will serve as the basis for discussion in chapter eight.

Finally, the mythos functions to transform existence. It is in this respect teleological. To assert this of the Christian mythos is to be reminded that there is no severance of *theoria* and *praxis*, of theology and ethics, of faith and obedience, of hearing and doing, of indicative and imperative. Any attempt to understand the Christian mythos then must involve us in a consideration of its meaning for action in the world.

This then is what is involved in identifying Christianity as a religion and in understanding its fundamental expression to function as a mythos. This will have important consequences for sorting out the tasks of theology.

In discussing the modes of the religious imagination it was noted that mythos refers to all the products of the religious imagination which function paradigmatically for a community. It is important now to give a more concrete specification of the Christian mythos. The first task is to identify the reference of the term mythos to Christianity.

THE COMPOSITION OF THE CHRISTIAN MYTHOS

The term mythos is admittedly somewhat flexible and it is intended that it retain some ambiguity. This ambiguity is necessary, first, because a variety of documents, practices, symbols, and assertions are included in it. Second, the relative importance of these things shifts from one group of Christians to another, as do also the limits of what is actually regarded as functioning in the ways appropriate to a mythos. Third, some things function as a part of the mythos which are not officially regarded by the community as a part of it. These variables will become more clear as we proceed.

The term mythos includes first of all the kerygma, that is, the essential structure of the Christian proclamation. This, of course, is subject to variable expression but concerns the significance of Jesus' life, death, and resurrection as the locus of God's presence and activity on behalf of humanity.

The elaboration and application of this kerygmatic structure within the communities of faith leads to the production of documents within and for these communities, some of which are subsequently taken to be apostolic (that is, deriving from or authentically representing the proclamation and teaching of the earliest communities) and therefore acquire the functions of the mythos. These documents, together with the writings which Judaism regarded as normative, were taken by the Christian community to be canonical. Thus, Scripture takes its place as a fundamental part of the mythos. The development of the canon of Scripture is a long and complex process which is, however, very instructive for us of the nature of the authority of the elements of the mythos. It is, of course, a process which is fundamentally political in nature, for it involves the determination of just which documents do in fact a) inform the life of faith of the various communities constitutive of the church and b) may be taken by the entire community to be expressive rather than distortive of the common faith (one test for which being their apostolicity as previously noted). The first list of such documents was put forward by Marcion and was subsequently deemed to be inadequate—not because it included too much, but because it included too little. One gains from this the impression that the concern was to have a sufficiently broad and diverse canon so as to accommodate the entire community without abandoning the various tests of authenticity. The church recognizes the authority with which these documents are functioning. But the pronouncement of a canon also represents the consensus of the community out of which (at a much earlier stage) they have come.

A third element constitutive of the mythos is the ritual or liturgy of the community. The way in which materials in both Old and New Testaments are derived from the worship of the community has been brought most forcefully to our attention by form-criticism. Moreover the determination of the canon was in great part a determination of which documents should be read from in public worship. But more than this is intended by the inclusion of ritual within the Christian mythos. The liturgies of the churches by their dramatic and public form and their regular repetition do far more to pattern perception and orient existence than is often recognized in Protestantism. This is especially true of those ritual forms which have been set apart as sacramental, by which is meant that a) they pattern the perception of community; b) they stem from the foundation of the community; c) they convey what they represent. Endless debate has been occasioned by attempts to formulate the precise working of (c) and the exact determination of (b). No survey or settlement of this dispute is possible here. All that is important at this point is to make clear that these ritual, and especially sacramental, forms do in fact function for wide sectors of the community past and present, to represent, orient, communicate, and transform existence, and that they do so in such a way as not merely to repeat but to supplement kerygmatic and scriptural elements of the mythos.

A fourth element constituting the Christian mythos is made up of decrees and subsequent theological materials which function to provide rules for the interpretation of other elements of the mythos and to take on in fact, if not in theory, the functions of the mythos for subsequent generations and communities. The decisions and decrees of the ecumenical councils, for example, serve as hermeneutical keys for the right (i.e., authoritative for the community as a whole) interpretation, elaboration, and application of Scripture and kerygma. Some of these decrees eventuate in creedal formulations which play a significant role in worship and provide a basis for subsequent theological reflection. (I have in mind here, for example, the way in which the so-called Apostles' Creed serves as a basis for theological commentary in much the same way as Romans or Galatians also do.)

The reflection by a theologian upon one or more elements of a received mythos may subsequently also function as an element of that mythos—itself acquiring a paradigmatic character. The writings of the Church Fathers clearly have played such a role, and the writings of Aquinas and Luther play such a role in significant sectors of the Christian community. Despite much Protestant emphasis upon *sola scriptura* it must be admitted that the writings (*scriptura*) of Luther have played a far more decisive role for faith and reflection in communities deriving from him than have, say, the Apocalypse of John or the Epistle of James. This in no way settles the theological question of *sola scriptura* but it does indicate that such materials do in fact function as elements of the mythos.

Now the reason for some ambiguity in the reference of the term mythos should be becoming clear. As a Protestant theologian, I tend to think primarily of Scripture when speaking of a mythos, but not exclusively so. Moreover, I think of it as arising from and directed toward proclamation. But other elements are also fundamental to and constitutive of the mythos and this introduces ambiguity as now one, now another of these elements comes nearer the center of discussion. Further ambiguity is introduced by the considerable difference among Christian communities regarding the precise enumeration of elements constitutive of each category. Is the Apocrypha canonical? Are there two or seven or no sacraments, and in what sense? Is Luther, Augustine, Aquinas, Kierkegaard, John Bunyan, or Mary Baker Eddy to be taken as forming the perception and lifestyle of a community? These kinds of questions indicate the difficulty of providing a precise definition of the limitations of the mythos which will be generally applicable.

The definition which I have given of a mythos is an entirely functional one. It is from some such sense of the functional nature of authority in the elements of the mythos that such questions as "why can't something be added to the canon?" arise. Now, as I have indicated, some things do get added to the mythos but their addition is not usually intentional and it is often not even publicly affirmed. It does, however, seem to me that it is helpful to restrict the category of mythos in three ways: first, that whatever is rightly taken to be an element of the mythos perform the functions indicated not for an individual, an elite, or a sect, but rather for a substantial community enduring through time and across generations. This communal restriction is, I think, sufficiently grounded in our discussion of religion to be clear if not self-evident. A second restriction, which merely entails making explicit what is implicit in each of the functions, is that nothing should be considered a part of the mythos which does not specifically have to do with what has been called the conjunction of sacred and profane. This religious restriction may be helpful in allowing us to distinguish between world view and faith without denying that the latter does entail the former. It would therefore be inexact to refer to Marxism as a mythos although it does in many respects function as one. Notice, however, that this religious restriction does not exclude but specifically includes the worldly, secular and profane, but precisely as that is engaged by the sacred. The third restriction is somewhat more difficult to formulate but nevertheless important to indicate. It may be called the "Christian restriction." Briefly put, it would indicate that not everything which meets all of the above tests may be regarded as an element in the Christian mythos. I know of no more adequate formulation of this restric-

tion than the one which Luther applied to the writings of the New
Testament itself, namely, that which bears Christ. And I am
perfectly aware that that must seem to be a hopelessly vague criterion. It is in any case not something to be specified in advance of
theological reflection. Its purpose here is to indicate that the
Christian mythos is determined by its reference to the history,
person, and significance of Jesus. Some consideration will be
given to the relationship of this resolute particularity to the intention of universality in a subsequent chapter.

We should note, finally, that there is a sense in which there is
more than one Christian mythos. This has to do not simply with
variations in what is taken to be a part of the mythos, but rather
with the way in which even the most basic elements are in tension
with one another. Herbert Braun has rightly pointed to the
irreconcilable diversity even with respect to a determination of
the significance of Jesus in the New Testament materials.[11] This
very basic tension should not be covered over by an attempt to
harmonize which only distorts everything equally. This internal
tension is precisely a crucial and constitutive feature of the Christian mythos which by its diversity and flexibility of expression has
been adaptable to divergent times, cultures, and circumstances. It
is that which has, moreover, made the Christian mythos particularly
resistant to a reduction to a precise party-line, as Marcion himself
very early discovered. Whatever unity may be referred to by
Luther's aphorism about that which bears Christ, it is not reducible
to a shared body of opinion expressible in univocal propositions.
It is, therefore, this very tension which has provoked theological
reflection and chastened the results of that reflection. Any attempt,
therefore, to specify the content or even the essential structure of
the Christian mythos stands inevitably under the sign of provisionality.

Having thus warned the reader of the provisionality of such an
effort, it is nevertheless important to give here some indication of
what I take to be the structural particularity of the Christian
mythos. This must be done, even at the risk of departing from
methodological concerns in order to give some indication of what
I take to be particularly significant features of that mythos. This
can be done only from the distance appropriate to an introduction
(as though discerning a mountain range from afar) but with the
conviction appropriate to an invitation.

THE STRUCTURE OF THE CHRISTIAN MYTHOS

In what follows I will adumbrate some of the features of the Christian mythos which are structural rather than doctrinal in character. This cannot pretend to be a universally accepted analysis of that mythos. This does, however, represent an attempt to discern the structure of the mythos from the standpoint of one who is concerned with the imagination. They should serve as a way of inquiring whether some work of art, literature, theology, or philosophy is informed by that mythos altogether apart from its actual content. While it cannot be helped that some of my theological biases will peek out beneath the edges of the exposition, it may nevertheless serve to give the reader some idea of the specificity of the Christian mythos (its peculiarity) and thus of the imagination informed by that mythos, whether that imagination is tutored to the disciplines of poetry or theology, the writing of novels, or the writing of liturgies. Each of these elements derives from the circumstance that the Christian mythos is focused upon the life and destiny of the man Jesus. Moreover, these elements have particular relevance for considerations of theological method.

Concreteness. The first characteristic of the Christian imagination is its typical emphasis upon the particular, the concrete, and the actual, as opposed to the sheerly universal, the infinite, and the bizarre. William Lynch in his book *Christ and Apollo*[12] develops this contrast across a wide range of modern literature and theology, and Erich Auerbach notes a similar impact of the Judeo-Christian tradition upon literature in his monumental study of the literary imagination, *Mimesis.*[13]

What is involved in this contrast—which might be termed provisionally a Christian realism—is a positive valuation of the specifically human in all of its ordinariness and actuality. This is in contrast to a Gnostic imagination with its fascination for the infinite and abhorrence of the finite and limited. It may also be contrasted with the superstitious imagination which is characterized by its fascination for the bizarre, the miraculous, the extraordinary.

This characteristic emphasis, like many others, is one which Christianity inherits from Judaism. It receives its particular impetus, however, from the assertion of the full presence of God in the fully human Jesus. The structure of this type of assertion is paralleled by the discernment of the presence of grace in bread,

wine, and water, that is, in the common ingredients of human life
altogether. It is further paralleled by the special emphasis upon
children, the poor, and the simple, as people of God, which plays
such an important role in the imagination of the medieval period.
These and similarly patterned perceptions derive from the image
of the full presence of the sacred in the life of Jesus. Throughout
its history Christianity has waged a battle (not always successful)
against the docetic denial of this fundamental conjunction of the
sacred with the finite, common, and human. It is a battle which
is not simply theological in nature but also plays a fundamental
role in the life of the literary and artistic imagination.

Temporality. A second structural element of the Christian
mythos is its emphasis upon time. There are styles of imagination,
religious and otherwise, for which time is the great enemy. Time,
thus viewed, is given expression in Whitehead's phrase that "time
is a perpetual perishing."[14] The brief instant of the present is already receding into the gaping maw of an all consuming past which
yields its prey "never more." Passing into the past is a passing
away. The present is reduced to a razor edge of the moment poised
between the abysmal void of a dead past and the onrushing threat
of an unreal future—a future which holds only the final fate of
passing irretrievably into the tomb of yesterday.

Recoiling from time, the imagination may assume several patterns, the most typical being the "Myth of the Eternal Now" and
the "Myth of the Eternal Recurrence." Both may and do function
in the same way as the Christian mythos does, but they are distinguished from it by their denial of time.

The myth form of the eternal now is characteristic of various
forms of mysticism, some of the higher forms of religious medita-
tion of the East. It influences romantic poetry and, to a degree,
the theology of Barth, Bultmann, and Tillich. In the myth of
the eternal now the imagination recoils from the temporal flux to
enter into the timeless moment and the equally timeless eternal.
In the moment, as *krisis*, one penetrates into the timeless realm,
thereby overcoming the fate of passage. Here there is no possibility of approximation or development. There is either the eternal
now or there isn't, and each moment calls for a repetition of decision whereby one recoils from time into the eternal. One may
either persist in this dialectic or see time from the perspective of
the eternal as an illusion, as in some forms of Idealism and
Buddhism.

The myth form of the eternal recurrence is a different sort of recoil from temporality. It is characteristic of much primitive religion—especially as it develops in agrarian settings. Here time is essentially cyclic and may be patterned on the seasonal cycle of nature. While the symbol may be the most appropriate representation of the eternal now, the ritual seems to be the most appropriate representation of the eternal recurrence.[16] The cycle of birth, maturation, parenthood, and death is thus correlated with the pattern of seasonal succession. Most typically, the myths and rituals of such a form represent the time of origin or beginning as the foundational reality to which the hearer of the myth or participant in the ritual is made contemporary. Myths of the transmigration of souls provide a significant variation upon the mythic pattern of eternal recurrence.

The temporal structure of the Christian mythos may be understood not as a denial of or recoil from time but as a celebration of time as grace. Events of time are fundamentally unrepeatable. Thus there is not a *dying* and *rising* God but the worship of a *crucified* and *resurrected* Lord. The past is indeed remembered but it is not actually repeated. The greatest temptation in the Christian mythos to a sense of repetition is in the ritual, but even here there is normally a clear priority of the unrepeatable.

There is a further tendency for time to be understood as incremental in which the events of the past or present are the womb out of which the future is born. This is related to the eschatological structure of the Christian mythos which will be dealt with further on. The notions of progress and evolution are secular equivalents of this form of the Christian imagination.

What is generally in view here is the historical structure of the Christian mythos. This is, however, a very complex structure and will concern us in the three sections which follow, suggesting as they do the place in the Christian mythos for past, future, and present.

Past. It is frequently maintained that the Christian story deals with history rather than myth. This is, I believe, a misleading distinction. It would be better perhaps to say that the Christian mythos is the transfiguration of events in history rather than the transfiguration of recurrent rhythms or natural cycles. In any case it is not history as such (in one of our several modern senses of history running from positivism to existentialism) with which the Christian faith is concerned, but with that in history which may be represented as the locus of revelation and redemption, or the point at which the sacred conjoins with the profane.

This point should be borne particularly in mind when attention is drawn to the way in which the mythos focuses upon Jesus. The Jesus thus focused upon is always and only Jesus as confessed by faith. Jesus is of interest even to the synopticist only insofar as he is the one who brings salvation (given the multiplicity of images from which that phrase generalizes). This, on the other hand, does not mean that for Jesus we are offered a substitute timeless myth which is wholly dissociated from Jesus himself. Jesus has been transfigured into the kerygma, but this kerygma and the materials which it orders are not generated *de novo* or *ex nihilo*. The given of which the mythos is a symbolic transformation is what happens in and through Jesus of Nazareth and it is precisely that given which is mediated in the mythos but only as transformed into the mythos. Therein lies both the possibility for and limitation upon the new quest for the historical Jesus. By tracing the various stages of the development of the mythos back to its earliest accessible layer such a quest hopes to discern the traces of that which the mythos represents.[17]

What proponents of the new quest were concerned to assert is a peculiar structure of the Christian mythos wherein it seems to differ significantly from others—namely, its pointing to an actual human being who lived at a particular time, died in a particular way, said and did certain kinds of things rather than others. If this peculiarity of structure is passed over when one speaks of the mythic or symbolic or kerygmatic nature of the New Testament materials, then a crucial feature is lost—namely, that of locating the event of salvation in history. But this feature is one of a *mythos*, i.e., that which gives expression to the presence of the sacred in such a way as to represent, orient, communicate, and transform existence for a community.

Now this is by way of asserting that the Christian mythos is historical in the sense of having reference to a particular past. It is not the anonymous past of the beginning or once upon a time nor the constructed past of fiction, but the named and more or less re-constructible past to which memory and historical criticism also refer.

There is a second and derivative sense in which the mythos may be characterized by the sense for the past, and that is the way in which the mythos is transmitted through the history of the community. It is intriguing to note here that a part of the canon is the *Acts of the Apostles*. This suggests the role which the history of the community plays in the mythos itself—something perhaps even more clearly true of Judaism. The tendency of some forms of biblicism to leap from the present to the time of the Bible (whatever that might designate) is, in the sense being stressed here, *unhistorical*. The Christian mythos is received from the past in the sense of being transmitted through the history of a community. This history does not itself usually function mythically—at least, not officially—but its very significance in the community is derived from the structure of the mythos itself insofar as it emphasizes the historical. This is why church history is taught in the seminary—because the history of the community is taken to be constitutive of that community and hence of the self-understanding of one within that community, and thus informative of the way in which one appropriates and interprets that mythos which founds and sustains both the community and the individual interpreter.

Future. The Christian mythos emphasizes not only the past but also the future. We noted in discussing the modes of the religious imagination that apocalyptic plays a significant part in the Christian mythos. This must now be clarified.

The characteristic reference of apocalyptic is the future, and in this lies its specific difference from the myth of origin. The *form* which this reference takes is typically that of the written account of a vision. In the time of the emergence of Christianity there had developed a considerable body of such literature with a fairly well defined vocabulary of typical images: resurrection, judgment, messiah, cosmic transformation, etc. These three: reference, form, and vocabulary are found together in the New Testament only in the *Book of Revelation*. If we exclude the form but look for material expressing the reference to the future in the vocabulary of apocalyptic, the increase in material is great and it becomes clear how significant a role is played by apocalyptic in the New Testament and thus in the mythos generally.[18]

The proclamation of Jesus announcing the kingdom of God is clearly apocalyptical in the general sense that we are using that term here. Indeed, it was the recognition of the way in which the reference to the kingdom of God was thoroughly permeated by eschatological concerns which precipitated a crisis in modern New

Testament scholarship at the turn of the century. Johannes Weiss[19] and subsequently Albert Schweitzer[20] noted that Jesus himself was thoroughly eschatological in his proclamation and expectation of an imminent catyclysm in which the kingdom of God would be actualized. This emphasis runs throughout the New Testament and is variously muted (Luke), translated (John), and emphasized (Apocalypse) by various writers of the New Testament and is fully present in the letters of Paul.

Apocalyptic imagery is frequently found to be the most distressing to the literal-minded—either because they accept it literally and go off the theological deep-end, or because they find it unintelligible or repugnant as literal assertion and therefore must reject or minimize it. Both attitudes are equally mistaken and arise from a misapprehension of the nature of religious language. It has reference to the future but not in the sense of purporting to be next year's newspaper, nor is it a prediction in the sense of a projection of a trajectory from the past through the present into the future. It is the representation of the future as the fundamental locus of the presence of the sacred.

So determinative of the structure of the earliest forms of the mythos is this that it qualifies the meaning of everything. Thus, for example, the assertion of the Lordship of Christ may be read not as announcing something that *has happened* but something which *will* happen. Jesus is not only the one who has come but also, and perhaps more importantly, the one who will come. Thus the horizon of expectation assigns to the past the meaning of a promise.[21] So intimately are promise and fulfillment, past and future linked together in the mythos that it produces a characteristic tension of already and not-yet which patterns the perspective of Paul particularly, and of other New Testament writers generally.[22] Thus memory fuels expectation which in turn remembers because of what it expects.

It is this stress upon anticipation and expectation which also serves to characterize the mythos as historical. Where what is real has already happened and nothing is to be expected but its fading flow or recurrent re-presentation, then the nerve of all historical interest is cut.[23] Time itself takes on intrinsic meaning only if the future is greater than and different from the past, for it is only in terms of difference that time can be experienced, and in terms of a difference which is grace that it can take on religious meaning. Thus the Christian mythos engenders not only a faith which remembers and relies upon what it remembers, but a hope which expects and anticipates that which it expects.

Present. Past and future, memory and expectation both form and inform the present. It is in the present that one remembers and hopes, and it is the present which is constituted in its meaning by memory and hope. Thus constituted, the present is the time of love.

The Christian view of love stands equally opposed to the Stoic and Epicurean envisagement of persons as fundamentally discreet and autonomous individuals on the one hand, and to the romantic envisagement of relationship as immediacy on the other hand. I will refer to three ways in which this is expressed in the Christian mythos: a) rituals of relationship; b) ethics of recognition; c) politics of compassion.

The ritual of relationship *par excellence* in the Christian imagination is the sacrament of the Lord's Supper. In the sacrament the foundational past is remembered and the eschatological anticipation is enacted. But in addition it represents the body of Christ as the symbolic expression not only of Jesus' death but also of the unity of the community. The ritual does not merely represent a given matrix of relatedness but entails the transformation of that matrix —the establishment of a community. Mutual participation in the sacred as mediated by bread and wine establishes a community of participation in the existence of one another. The basis for this participation is not friendship or affinity, but the ritual itself in which—imaginatively—we become one body.

We should notice here that baptism also is a ritual through which one is brought into relation to the sacred and to a community. In the case of infant baptism the person is brought into this relationship altogether apart from the illusion of choice or merit, thus asserting that the relationship mediated through the ritual has priority over awareness, intentionality, or achievement. This is a vigorous insistence upon the way in which meaning is donated to existence from outside itself by way of the enactment of the mythos in the community.

The ethics of recognition depends in part upon this implicit universalism. It depends upon the connection between that act of belief whereby we recognize our own existence as represented by the mythos, and the way in which that mythos thus patterns our perception of all human beings. The description of judgment in Matthew 25 links together the recognition of oneself as recipient of grace to the recognition of the need of the other as placing one under obligation deriving from the sacred. This makes a limitation upon one's responsibility for the need of the other impossible. Moreover, as both the story of judgment and the parable of the Good Samaritan make clear, the need of the other is recognized as just that need which it is. Hunger, sickness, imprisonment, are not allegories for some purely spiritual need. The ethic of recognition therefore is both radical (no limit upon responsibility) and social (no allegorizing of human need). Like the rituals of relationship, it places stress upon participation in the existence, meaning, and plight of the other while denying immediacy.

The politics of compassion points to the consequences of identifying the oppressed as the peculiar people of God. Compassion in this context means identification with and participation in the agony and pain of those who are dispossessed. The special emphasis which is placed by the Judeo-Christian tradition upon the poor, the exiled, and the outcast has been brought into new prominence by the work of Ernst Bloch and Jürgen Moltmann in Germany as well as by recent books on Black theology in the United States. Here it becomes clear how memory (exodus, crucifixion) and hope (messianic banquet, city of God) come together to focus upon the present as the place in which love is enacted in such a way as to transform the present into a prolepsis or anticipation of that which is to be. It should moreover make clear that the designation of the present as the time of love in no way entails a retreat from the world into the personal and intimate.

This all too brief survey should serve nonetheless as an indication of what I take to be fundamental structural or formal elements of the Christian mythos. I have made no attempt to be exhaustive or to maintain theological neutrality. The list of structural elements should therefore be taken as a provisional indication of some significant features of the Christian mythos which may serve as a backdrop against which to consider the tasks of theological reflection.

THE "WHAT" OF THEOLOGICAL REFLECTION

We have now come to the point of being able to say with some hope of being understood that theology is a reflection upon the

Christian mythos. This assertion must be distinguished from alternative conceptions of the object or the what of theological inquiry. Theology has been variously supposed to be 1) a reflection upon the being of God; 2) a reflection upon faith; 3) a reflection upon the beliefs and attitudes of a community; 4) a reflection upon the Word of God. While there is important truth in each of these assertions, they each distort in advance the task of theology.

That theology is a reflection upon the being of God is perhaps the most widespread view.[24] It assumes the immediacy of reflection to ultimate reality as one region of reality among others to which it may advert, albeit the most fundamental such region. This, however, constitutes a misunderstanding: first, because that which religion names the sacred is present only as mediated through the symbol or myth; and, second, because the sacred as thus given to experience is given only in conjunction with its other—the profane reality of world and existence. There are two ways in which God is taken as the immediate object of awareness and reflection —mysticism and philosophy. While both may play a role in theological reflection, they are not themselves theological in the sense being developed here. The truth contained in this understanding of theology is that theology does have to do with the ultimate reality which it names God and which we have been calling the sacred. In this it differs from the modern historical and natural sciences (and from philosophy insofar as it models itself upon them) which methodologically exclude considerations of ultimacy from their purview. But access to this reality is always indirect for Christian theology—always mediated by the disclosure of the sacred in time as represented by the mythos. This is not to deny the validity of the mystical or metaphysical concern with God but only to distinguish it from theology.

That theology is a reflection upon faith or upon existence in faith is a characteristic view of much contemporary theology.[25] Unlike the first, philosophical view, it emphasizes the concern of theological reflections with actual human existence. This is its great merit by which it is distinguished also from other views we shall consider. Whatever its other antecedents, it does derive, in part, from Schleiermacher's understanding of theology as a reflection upon the religious consciousness of absolute dependence.[26] Its close affinity with the first view may be indicated by saying that faith is the subjective correlate in existence to the reality of God.

Again there can be no question that theology is concerned with existence in faith, but this existence is never sheerly given as an immediate datum for reflection. Rather it is mediated to reflection only by way of the images, symbols, and narratives of the mythos. Thus while theology is concerned with existence and existence in faith, its approach is indirect—by way of the mythos. For the mythos determines the forms which that existence will take in expression and action.

That theology is a reflection upon the beliefs and attitudes of the Christian community is a view which seeks to counteract the individualism of the preceding two views and thus to emphasize the social character of Christianity. The necessity for such a qualification was already seen by Schleiermacher[27] but it received fullest expression in Ritschl.[28] It is right in asserting that faith emerges in and is derived from a community and that the representations or images of that faith are fundamentally collective. Unfortunately, however, this definition surrenders any norm by which the community itself might be corrected and comes close to dissolving theology into sociology as previously theology was dissolved into psychology or ontology. It can only function insofar as the community is tacitly assumed to be commensurate with its mythos. But this would make the phenomena of prophets and reformers (and even theologians) impossible. Thus this definition needs to be completed by reference to a mythos which creates and sustains that community but which also stands over against it as a prod towards transformation.

That theology is a reflection upon the Word of God is a view put forward by Karl Barth. It corrects the first view by pointing to the mediated character of theology's concern with God (i.e, through revelation). It corrects the second by pointing to that by virtue of which there is faith (thus eliminating the narcissism of faith's self-preoccupation). It corrects the third by supplying a norm in terms of which the community may be corrected without denying the communal and ecclesiastical character of theology as church dogmatics. Nevertheless, it is a misleading and inappropriate designation of the what of theological reflection. In his eagerness to avoid the absolutizing of the subject concealed in the second position (faith as the what), Barth virtually eliminates reference to existence, thus leading to the charge of his critics that his view represents a kind of revelational positivism which seems oblivious to the situation of the actually existing Christian. More-over, Barth's reliance upon a doctrine of the Trinity and Incarnation as the starting point of his reflection subordinates reflection to ecclesiastical formulations whose appropriateness and intelligibility it has yet to evaluate. That one must begin at *some* point with a recognition which constitutes a pre-understanding (in the sense of the hermeneutical circle) of what is to be understood, I do not deny. But the specification of that as any particular dogma or all of them together seems altogether arbitrary. If it is true that one must believe in order to understand, it is also true that one must understand in order to believe. This necessary dialectic is fore-shortened by Barth's definition of theology as reflection upon the Word of God.

Thus far we have looked at alternatives to considering the mythos as the what of theological reflection. We may now consolidate the argument of this first part of the essay by attempting a positive though preliminary characterization of what is involved in taking the mythos to be the object of theological inquiry.

The Christian mythos determines the horizon of meaning within which it may be understood—it locates theological reflection. This it does in such a way as to incorporate the definitions of theology which we have previously considered. The question of ultimacy is raised but in relation to the mythos which only knows of ultimacy as the sacred which bestows meaning and fills being. The question of existence is raised but from the standpoint of the mythos which represents and orients that existence. The question of collective and social meaning is raised but in relation to and over against the mythos which grounds the community. Thus much is gained which Barth sought to gain by his doctrine of the Word of God—a guard against the reduction of theology to philosophy, psychology, or sociology—without paying the inflated fee which Barth demands for entrance into the hermeneutical circle of theological reflection.

The term Christian mythos reminds us that the object of theo-logical reflection is founded in the imagination and thus requests of us that we attend to the specifically symbolic character of its expression. In this way the inappropriateness of a literal reduction of its language is noted and the point of contact between theology and other disciplines which reflect upon symbolic expression is maintained. We are reminded of the distinction between the symbolic expression and its given as well as of the relationship between them through the principle of the symbolic transformation of the given. The tendency to confuse the imaginative representation with its given present in descriptions of the object of theology as revelation or the Gospel, the Word of God, or God is thereby guarded against.

To speak of a mythos as the object of theological reflection points to the connection between Christianity and other religions and reminds us that what we call the Christian mythos is, like the mythos of other religious communities, the representation of the sacred in our world in such a way as to represent, orient, communicate, and transform our existence in the world. That the Christian mythos performs these functions in common with the images and symbols of other religions will provide, then, important clues for the appropriate means of interpreting the meaning of Christianity. Moreover, the term mythos permits us to include, as the object of reflection, a range of materials, such as liturgy, sacraments, and the history of theological reflection which function as mythos but which might be overlooked or forgotten if we simply described the object of our reflection as the Bible or the Christian story.

Finally, the term Christian mythos as the designator of the object of theological reflection enables us to point to the peculiar structure of this mythos without abrogating the categories derived from the phenomenological investigation of the imagination generally, or of the religious imagination particularly.

NOTES

1. Anders Nygren criticizes Bultmann and others for importing the term myth into a consideration of the kerygma in which it has no home. This is, he asserts, a land of category mistake. Nygren's argument is not a fully cogent one since it rests upon a misunderstanding of the term myth in Bultmann. In any case it does not impinge upon the way in which the category of mythos is used in this essay. For Nygren's position on methodological issues (which provides a useful contrast to the perspective I am working out here) cf. *Meaning and Method,* trans. Philip S. Watson. (Philadelphia: Fortress Press, 1972).

2. For Barth's argument cf. his commentary *The Epistle to the Romans,* trans. Edwyn Hoskyns. (London: Oxford University, 1933), pp. 229 ff.

3. Bonhoeffer, *Letters and Papers from Prison,* enlarged edition, ed. Eberhard Bethge. (New York: Macmillan, 1972), p. 28.

4. *Ibid.,* p. 285.

5. For an elaboration of some of the implications of Bonhoeffer's thought cf. G. Ebeling, "The Non-religious Interpretation of Biblical Concepts" in *Word and Faith,* trans. James W. Leitch. (Philadelphia:

Fortress Press, 1963), pp. 98–161, and Heinrich Ott, *Reality and Faith* (Philadelphia: Fortress Press, 1972).

6. Examples of such argumentation may be found in Harvey Cox, *The Secular City* (New York: Macmillan, 1965), and in Paul Van Buren, *The Secular Meaning of the Gospel: based on an analysis of its meaning* (New York: Macmillan, 1963).

7. Most notably Altizer's *The Gospel of Christian Atheism* (Philadelphia: Westminster, 1966).

8. Rudolph Bultmann, *Theology of the New Testament*, trans. K. Grobel (New York: Scribners, 1951), I, p. 191.

9. John 5:25.

10. This assertion is parallel to Tillich's assertion that religion designates a depth dimension in all spheres of human life and culture. Cf. Tillich's *Theology of Culture*, ed. R. C. Kimball (New York: Oxford, 1964).

11. Cf. Herbert Braun, "The Meaning of New Testament Christology," trans. Paul J. Achtemeier in *Journal for Theology and Church*, Vol. V (New York: Harper & Row, 1968), pp. 89–127.

12. William Lynch, *Christ and Apollo* (New York: Sheed and Ward, 1960).

13. Erich Auerbach, *Mimesis: The Representation of Reality in Western Literature*, trans. Willard Trask (Garden City: Doubleday, 1957), esp. pp. 1–19.

14. A. N. Whitehead, *Process and Reality* (New York: Harper, 1960), p. 517.

15. For the elaboration of positions which correspond to this structure cf. Rudolph Bultmann, *History and Eschatology* (Edinburgh: University Press, 1957) and Karl Barth, *The Resurrection of the Dead*, trans. J. J. Stenning (London: Hodder & Stoughton, 1953).

16. Alan Watts, *Myth and Ritual in Christianity* (Boston: Beacon, 1968), is an interesting argument for the primacy of such a view of time in the Christian liturgy.

17. For an emphasis upon the necessity of such a quest cf. Ernst Käsemann, "The Problem of the Historical Jesus" in *Essays on New Testament Themes*, trans. W. J. Montague (London: SCM, 1964), pp. 15–47. It should be noted that Käsemann knows only a timeless and therefore anti-historical myth which he contrasts absolutely with the historical kerygma. For a discussion of the quest inaugurated by Käsemann cf. James M. Robinson, *A New Quest of the Historical Jesus* (London: SCM Press, 1959). For a discussion of the limitations of such a quest cf. Van A. Harvey's *The Historian and the Believer* (New York: Macmillan, 1966), pp. 164 ff.

18. For a survey of the research into the nature and significance of apocalyptic cf. Klaus Koch, *The Rediscovery of Apocalyptic* (Naperville: Allenson, 1972).

19. Johannes Weiss, *Jesus' Proclamation of the Kingdom of God,* trans. R. M. Miers and D. L. Holland (Philadelphia: Fortress Press, 1971).

20. Albert Schweitzer, *The Quest of the Historical Jesus*, trans. W. Montgomery, 3rd ed. (London: A. & C. Black, 1951).

21. Jürgen Moltmann, *Theology of Hope* (New York: Harper & Row, 1967). Wolfhart Pannenberg, *Theology and the Kingdom of God*, ed. R. J. Neuhaus (Philadelphia: Westminster, 1969).

22. Rudolph Bultmann, *Theology of the New Testament*, I, pp. 274 ff.

23. Jürgen Moltmann, *Hope and Planning*, trans. Margaret Clarkson (New York: Harper & Row, 1971), pp. 56–100 ("Exegesis and the Eschatology of History").

24. This definition of theology is taken up by Aquinas in his *Summa Theologica* Part I, Chapter 1, question 7.

25. Cf. Fritz Buri, *Theology of Existence*, trans. H. H. Oliver and G. Onder (Greenwood, South Carolina: Attic Press, 1965).

26. Friedrich Schleiermacher, *The Christian Faith, op. cit.*, pp. 12–18.

27. Friedrich Schleiermacher, *Brief Outline on the Study of Theology*, trans. Terrence N. Tice (Richmond: John Knox, 1966), pp. 20 ff.

28. Albrecht Ritschl, *The Christian Doctrine of Justification and Reconciliation*, trans. H. R. Mackintosh and A. B. Macaulay (Clifton, New Jersey: Reference Book, 1966), p. 6.

29. For Barth the task of dogmatics is to test the proclamation of the church against the criterion of God's Word. Cf. *Church Dogmatics*, Vol. I, Part I, trans. G. T. Thomson (Edinburgh: T. T. Clark, 1936), pp. 79 ff.

PART II

THE DIALECTIC OF
THEOLOGICAL REFLECTION

Having achieved some clarity about the object of theological reflection it is possible for us to give some attention to the ways in which one may profitably reflect upon that object. These ways of reflecting are termed here the "how" of theological reflection. This should not, however, be taken to mean that a recipe or operator's manual is about to be supplied, the careful adherence to which will automatically produce an adequate theological system. Instead I will propose certain ways in which the theologian may attempt to reconcile quite different perspectives in order to render a more fully adequate theological judgment. These perspectives will be presented as a series of polar opposites, the harmonization of which in relation to the Christian mythos will guide reflection. Now it is necessary to clarify the procedure in advance in order to give the reader prior notice of the terrain through which we will be passing.

The first thing to be noticed and emphasized here is that the manner of thinking about the Christian mythos is one which is derived from the nature of that mythos itself. This is only to say that the method of inquiry must be related to the subject matter of that inquiry. It would do us little good to apply mathematics to the analysis of dreams, or to use Freud's *Interpretation of Dreams* as a guide to understanding the movement of planets. Part of the reason for having given so much attention to the nature of the Christian mythos is to guide our consideration of method by a more adequate understanding of the subject matter to which that method is to be applied. In theology as in every intellectual inquiry we must consent to learn our method from the subject matter itself. One way of testing what will be maintained in the following chapters is to ask whether what is being suggested is commensurate with the nature of the Christian mythos as discussed in Part One.

The method which is proposed here is not intended as a strait-jacket for thought, nor as a technique which may be employed dispassionately or objectively. Instead I invite you to take up a series of perspectives from which to view both the mythos and human existence. These perspectives are intended to open up for view wider horizons of meaning and understanding. While many theological issues traditionally part of a prolegomena will be dis-cussed here, they will always be discussed in relation to the char-acter of human existence. Thus problems like those of the authority and interpretation of Scripture and tradition will be discussed as analogues to the process of coming to terms with our own past which is fundamental to human health and growth. This is not intended as a gimmick to lure the reader through otherwise dry material but represents the true character of theological reflection—a reflection which can never be appropriately severed from the actual concern for the illumination of our own and one another's existence.

The perspectives from which to reflect upon the mythos are presented here in contrasting pairs: individual and communal, past and present, particular and universal, and so on. One of the things that I will attempt to show is that these pairs do belong together and that holding them together is a fruitful way of proceeding in reflecting upon the mythos and in reflecting about the character of our life. This activity of holding together contrasting perspectives may be called dialectical. It is in the nature of a conversation where the truth lies in neither side separately but emerges through their communictaion with one another. It is natural to want to avoid unnecessary complication and to stick to perspectives which have become habitual, but that is to condemn our reflection to a kind of monologue which loses in vigor and vitality more than it gains in simplicity and clarity. By holding contrasting perspectives together, moving from one to the other and seeking to harmonize them, theological reflection moves forward toward a fruitful and communicable understanding of the Christian mythos and thereby toward an understanding of existence as illumined by that mythos.

These contrasting perspectives are irreducible but they are not arbitrarily juxtaposed. They belong intimately together yet they cannot be reduced to a single term. This is what makes the reflection which moves between them necessarily dialectical. That should become clear as the presentation of these perspectives proceeds.

Chapter 6

Faith and Reflection

JERUSALEM AND ATHENS

If our task in this second part of our essay is to specify the manner and context of theological reflection, then clearly we must first justify what is otherwise simply presupposed—namely, the relation between conviction and reflection, between the immediacy of faith and the distancing of reflection. This relationship, sometimes characterized as the wedding of Athens and Jerusalem, produces a characteristic tension in theological discourse. Friends of one or the other partner of this perennial odd couple have regularly counseled divorce. Indeed, in the period following the Reformation, philosophy (representing Athens) and piety (representing Jerusalem) have each declared its own autonomy, thinking thereby to dissolve the tensions produced by what each has taken to be an unfruitful if not also an unholy alliance. Much of the confusion with respect to the nature of theological reflection is due to the fact that our intellectual context is largely influenced by the descendants of either pietism or enlightenment philosophy, who fail to recognize the necessity or even the character of that relationship between faith and reflection which helps to define the structure of any genuinely theological inquiry. Let us therefore seek to characterize this relationship more precisely.

The term faith denotes a relationship of immediacy, of dependence, and of participation. In this it is like such terms as trust and love. Indeed, these terms are often, with good cause, taken to be synonymous. Thus the relationship of faith is compared in the New Testament to the relationship which a child has to a loving parent.

Moreover, as the term is usually employed, faith refers to that conviction or set of convictions which constitute the most fundamental frame of reference for judgment and behavior in the world.

Faith as trust and faith as conviction are frequently set at odds.
So, for example, the understanding of faith as a relationship is
distinguished from belief in the truth of a certain set of propositions
in order to make clear the personal or existential character of faith.
The result, however, of such a sharp distinction is to sever faith
from any content whatever in such a way that a certain mysticism
becomes apparent in the retreat from articulate conviction. The
danger is even greater from the other side, however, when faith is
too readily identified with a propositional content. Here Biblicism,
Fundamentalism, and Orthodoxy sever faith from its relational
ground, leaving us with a faith reduced to historical assertions and
assent to those assertions.

In terms of our previous discussion, faith entails the recognition
of oneself and of reality through the perspective opened up by the
mtyhos and thus involves participation in the sacred and in the
world as encountered by sacrality, through the mediation of the
mythos. Apart from the mythos there is no relation to the sacred,
but through the mythos and the convictions which it evokes, one
is placed in relation to the sacred.

But whether faith be understood as trust or conviction (or, as
I am suggesting, as these together) it seems to remain in sharp
contrast to the critical reflective process which stands over against
its object (therefore not immediate to it) and subjects all convictions to that testing and probing which renders them inoperative
as convictions for the time of critical scrutiny. Critical reflection
seems to cut the nerve of conviction by its suspension of judgment.
Moreover, its movement of distancing interrupts and brings to an
end the immediacy characteristic of trust.

For this reason, faith has often discerned in critical reflection an
antagonist to whom every foothold must be denied. The impervi-
ous autonomy of reflection stands in this view in sharpest contrast
to the proper attitude of devotion and obedience. Thus, in the
name of faith the tasks of theological reflection may be eschewed.
The biblicist, for example, will oppose vigorously the advancement
of biblical scholarship which invokes the methods of critical examination. Fundamentalism will oppose the spirit of scientific inquiry
whose result might be to compel abondonment or serious revision
of the so-called fundamentals of faith. And orthodoxy admits of
only increasing refinement of the conceptual tools by which to
articulate the convictions of the Christian community, thus limiting

reflection to a supportive and elaborative function and allowing it
no critical function at all with respect to those convictions.

Now it must be admitted that there is an element of truth in the
opposition of faith to reflection. As we noted at the very beginning, reflection tends to sever itself from the density and life-giving
power of experience as mediated through imagination. It then
becomes abstract, objective, and manipulative. It may in the end
produce that objective-manipulative consciousness which invades
thought and life with numbing effect, making trust and involvement
impossible.

On the other hand, faith is itself committed to the reflective task
for reasons of its own not imposed upon it from outside but
emerging directly out of its own nature. The character of a mythos
itself, with its intention to interpret, orient, transform, and communicate existence, requires its continuous elaboration and application in any society where significant changes occur, if the mythos
is not to be simply abandoned. To be sure, the consequence of
this activity may be the continuous supplementation and alteration
of the mythos. This process has been illumined most helpfully by
an examination of the development of pre-scriptural traditions in
the Judeo-Christian tradition. Here the conviction that YHWH
was to be understood as Lord of history provided the impetus and
possibility for continuous development and re-interpretation of the
received mythos to meet altered circumstances. The reflective
process which may be discerned in the emergence of the Deuter-
onomist's historiography or the selective and elaborative process
discernible in the emergence of Johannine and Pauline theologies,
already shows that the mythos bears within itself the seeds of its
own development through reflective processes. It would have
been a repudiation of its own internal logic, therefore, for the
Christian community to have refused to seek to elaborate its
mythos in terms of the categories of the Hellenistic culture in
which it found itself. Thus, very early on the process of Helleni-
zation began (indeed before Paul), leading of necessity to the
encounter of Jerusalem with Athens, which in turn becomes constitutive of the structure and historical destiny of Christianity. To
have labeled this either mere historical accident or temptation of
the devil would have been a betrayal of the principal convictions
expressed in the mythos—namely, that history itself was the sphere
of the encounter with the sacred.

Nor is this the only reason for the necessity which drives faith to an appreciation for and employment of the reflective spirit. When faith sets itself against a critical examination of itself, it negates the distinction between faith (*Glaube*) and superstition (*Aberglaube*) so important to the Judeo-Christian tradition. Quite early in the experience of Israel the polemic against idolatry which receives normative expression in the first commandment functioned to incite a critique, not only of religious practices and beliefs among Israel's neighbors (and defecting Israelites), but also of Israel's own religious practices and beliefs, as a reading of the prophets sufficiently demonstrates. That the question of false prophets arose in this context indicates to what extent the existence of Israel's faith was closely bound up with a critical, and, indeed, self-critical, appraisal of those convictions which passed for fundamental.

This conjunction of faith wtih a critical reflection is similarly to be found wtih the emergence of Christianity. The conflict between Jesus and the Pharisees is, at least in part, a conflict within Judaism over the character of faith. Thus the question whether Jesus cast out demons through a league with Satan or by the power of God represents the way in which a critical principle is already at work in the formative stages of the Christian mythos. The necessity to "test the spirits" was thenceforth imposed upon Christianity no less than upon Judaism. The polemical spirit of Paul's letters shows how this critical appraisal became crucial to the task of establishing the Christian community.

Now this brief summary of the place of critical reflection could be much expanded and brought forward through the history of the Christian community. Certainly its place in the Reformation is sufficiently crucial to justify Tillich's habit of calling this critical reflection the Protestant principle. This designation, however, may obscure the deeper rootage of this principle in the Judeo-Christian tradition as well as fail to do justice to its presence at the heart of all communities which are successors to that tradition.

However it is designated, it is clear that critical reflection is crucial for faith, at least in the Judeo-Christian tradition. It is also clear that an attempt to separate faith from such reflection results in the collapse of the distinction between faith and superstition, thus associating faith with a naive gullibility (at best) or arrogant dogmatism. This is the meaning of the charge of obscurantism whose seriousness is accounted for by the fact that the obscurantist,

in the name of defending faith, does in fact strip faith of its chief
defense against unfaithfulness.

But at this point we have not resolved the tension between faith
and reflection. Instead it is only now becoming clear. For the
critical inquiry inspired by faith has as its chief aim the search for
fidelity, whereas the critical inquiry which we have inherited from
Athens seeks for intelligibility. From the side of the friends of
Athens it has seemed as though the quest for the faithful word has
frequently served to place a restriction upon the quest for a truly
intelligible word. Philosophy's declaration of independence from
theology during the time of the Enlightenment seemed to be necessitated by the determination to pursue all lines of inquiry regardless
of where they led. The resultant autonomy of philosophical and
scientific inquiry has given to modern Western culture its characteristic achievements and internal logic. The rhetoric with which
that autonomy was achieved, however, served to create the suspicion that faith was inimical to open and honest inquiry and to
persuade the sciences and philosophical reflection that they were or
could be entirely objective and without binding presuppositions,
thus implying an unbridgeable gulf between scientific inquiry (in
the broad sense) and religious faith.

The work of Michael Polanyi and Thomas Kuhn serves to show
how scientific inquiry even among the empirical sciences has been
made possible by something like a set of shared commitments
which do not derive from the evidence, but serve to provide the
perspective within which alone it is possible for evidence to appear.[1]
Now this contravenes the widespread assumption that scientific
inquiry may function independently of prior assumptions or convictions and thus be free of value judgments. That Christian theology was not prepared to abandon its convictions nor prepared to
dispense with judgment of value placed it in an unfavorable light.
Once it is clear, however, that this absolute difference does not
exist, the way is open at least in principle for a rapprochement
between faith and reflection.

The point which our argument has now reached is a convenient
place to warn against the way in which any set of presuppositions
or prior convictions may be ruled out of range of critical scrutiny
by labeling them "bliks." This term was introduced into the
discussion of philosophers regarding the logical status of sets of
presuppositions by R. M. Hare.[2] In the context of his argument

the use of the term serves to identify convictions which do not admit of falsifying evidence, yet which serve usefully to ground further assertions which are not so privileged. This argument then serves to create the impression that it is neither necessary nor possible to evaluate critically such convictions. The term itself may therefore be invoked to shift attention away from the critical examination of crucial convictions. It is quite right to point out, as Hare does, that there are some convictions for which empirical evidence is generally an inappropriate means of verifying or falsifying. This ought not to lead, however, to the supposition that critical inquiry is thus put at an end. Instead it is directed to discover more fruitful means of evaluating such assumptions than by means of a simple counting up of verifying or falsifying instances.[3]

Now it may seem odd at this point to insist upon the capacity of reflection to test and interrogate the imaginative representations from which it derives. The argument of this essay thus far has served to assert the priority of imagination (and specifically the mythos) over reflection. How is it then that it is possible now to assert the prerogatives of reflection? I have already indicated that the mythos itself gives rise to a kind of critical reflection which seeks to "test the spirits" in an ongoing struggle against idolatry and superstition. Thus there is an important sense in which the imaginative representations of the Judeo-Christian tradition tend to be self-relativizing—standing under the first commandment. It is for this reason that the reflection which is founded by the mythos is not simply elaborative (extending and applying to fresh circumstances a received mythos) but also critical (turning to interrogate even expressions of the mythos itself).

For there to be such a critical reflection it is clear that one must live in a world in which there are alternative ways of comprehending reality ultimately based upon different representations of reality. If, as I have already argued, there is no immediate access to the real, but only such access as is mediated in one way or another through its imaginative representation and transformation, then the only possibility for a critical interrogation of one set of such representations is through comparison with another such set. This requires a certain degree of pluralism. In fact, both Israel and Christianity emerged in precisely such pluralistic settings. Thus the imaginative forms peculiar to each and common to both were forged in the crucible of competing representations of reality, sacred and profane.

It was on account of the context in which it emerged in the Hellenistic world that Christian theology found itself increasingly employing the tools of an already existing philosophical vocabulary to carry out its internal tasks of critical reflection upon alternative interpretations of the Christian mythos. Thus out of its own internal necessity and external circumstance was consummated that wedding of Jerusalem and Athens. Theology is the child of this union.

It is largely due to this dual inheritance that theology may become a critical reflection upon the mythos at the same time that it is an interpretive elaboration of that mythos. In the appropriation of means for achieving conceptual clarity and precision from its philosophical heritage, theology is equipped to continue to perform its own critical (prophetic) inquiry into the adequacy or appropriateness of various expressions of Christian faith. When this critical reflection, however, is no longer fundamentally informed by the Christian mythos itself, then that reflection has ceased to be theology. Thus a precarious and dynamic balance moving between faith and reflection characterizes the peculiar dialectic of theological reflection.

We have seen that reflection and commitment are intimately bound to one another though, at the same time, capable of coming into conflict with one another. This produces the characteristic tension of theological reflection with its juxtaposition of faith and skepticism. There is no simple way of holding these two attitudes together, nor is one to expect an entire resolution of their allied though often competing demands. Theological reflection—insofar as it is *theological*—begins in commitment, however provisional and tentative, to understand by means of the mythos. . Insofar as it is critical *reflection,* however, it tests, probes, and interrogates each formulation of that understanding. Thus the theologian must with Anselm "believe in order to understand," but he must also undertake the opposite movement of an understanding which tests belief. There is in this something of what Paul Ricoeur calls the wager by which one suspends the claim of reflection to autonomy and has recourse to the symbol in order thereby to increase the scope and authenticity of reflection. But the wager works in the opposite direction as well when one who exists within the space created by the symbol wagers that the interrogation of the symbol through reflection will not weaken or destroy, but will give new vitality to the language of the mythos. The prospective theologian may come at this tension from any of several different perspectives but the very nature of the theological task will entail movement between them. This movement is harmonized by the intention to give reliable expression to what is truly real—an intention which is fully shared by faith and reflection.

We may now return to a model proposed earlier in chapter two when imagination was placed as the mediator between reality and reflection. That model was proposed as an alternative to the absolute autonomy of reflection and serves, especially when reflection has become associated with the juggernaut of objective-manipulative consciousness, to indicate the way in which reflection but precisely in order to reintegrate our reflection and understand-However, it would be a mistake for culture generally, and for theology particularly, to renounce reflection in the name of a return to the symbol. Such a return to the symbol is, of course, necessary, but precisely in order to reintegrate our reflection and understanding with the reality of our existence. Thus there is no inherent necessity for the emphasis upon either the image or the reflection to be at the expense of the legitimate prerogatives of the other. Theology has much to learn from the celebrators of the power of the religious imagination, but it cannot give up the insistence upon a careful quest for understanding in the midst of a legitimate enthusiasm for fantasy and imagination. Just such a danger looms upon our horizon as the temptation of becoming all too relevant to altered surroundings threatens to produce a theology which is no more than an echo of an emergent cultural style. If the first part of this essay was, in part, an argument for the humanizing character of the image and symbol, so this second part holds to the humanizing character of reflection—a reflection nourished and informed by those peculiar products of the human imagination which are being called the Christian mythos.

AIMS AND TASKS

I have attempted to argue for the possibility and importance of reflection which is in relationship to faith. While much of what follows will further clarify the nature of this reflection, it is important at this point to indicate some of the aims which it pursues

in relation to the mythos. This may be done perhaps most helpfully by a fourfold division roughly corresponding to our earlier
discussion of the functions of the mythos. There is nothing immu-
table or necessary in this division; it is only offered as an aid to
understanding.[4]

The first aim of theology is the critical testing of the authenticity
of expressions of the mythos. This function corresponds to the
prophetic and self-critical character of the mythos itself and may
be termed the *dogmatic task of theology*. Theology, as Barth
insisted, has the task of testing contemporary proclamation and
theological interpretation against the standard of what that preaching and interpretation take to be normative. While individual
theologians, and I am among them, may feel uneasy about engaging
in this sort of normative discipline, its importance should not be
underestimated. It was Dietrich Bonhoeffer who, to the horror
of his liberal colleagues in the ecumenical movement, sought to
rehabilitate the charge of heresy against those who acknowledged
the lordship of Hitler alongside of or in place of the lordship of
Christ.[5] The dangers of such a normative task are notorious and
have given the term dogmatic a pejorative odor. But a theology
which loses the possibility of distinguishing true from false teaching can no longer be responsible. (We will return to this theme in
discussing particularity and universality.) Theology has no privileged position of authority from which to pronounce upon true
and false doctrine—it can be here only a servant and guide for the
community. Its service consists in vigilance over the communication
of the mythos in order to warn against such distortions as would
empty the mythos of meaning or unawares exchange it for another.

A second aim of theology is so to clarify the import of the mythos
as to make it intelligible for contemporary experience. This may
be termed *the apologetic task of theology*. The difficulty to which
theology here responds is that the world of meaning indicated by
the Christian mythos may, for a wide range of reasons, seem
incomprehensible to those who live in a quite different world of
meaning. The apologetic task, therefore, involves an activity of
translation between different linguistic and symbolic worlds of
meaning or, as Tillich urged, a correlation of such worlds which
would facilitate the understanding of the mythos by one outside
its world of meaning.[6] The intention of the mythos we have seen
is to represent existence in such a way that one may recognize

oneself and one's world in it. The apologetic task of theology is to facilitate this recognition through an elaboration or interpretation of the representation. Bultmann's existential interpretation is a particularly important example of this apologetic function. Of course, the danger is always present that in pursuing this apologetic task theology may translate the mythos in such a way as to lose many of its important features and thus distort it. Hence the apologetic and dogmatic functions of theology are in need of close cooperation.

A third aim of theological reflection is the elaboration of the mythos in such a way as to make clear the interconnectedness and unity of reality as represented by the mythos. This may be called *the systematic task of theology.* We noted the intention of the mythos to orient existence within and in relation to the manifold dimensions of the human world, and it is this intention which is fulfilled or facilitated by systematic theology. This means, of course, that theology cannot be a discipline isolated from other disciplines which in their own way are concerned with an understanding of some region of existence and reality. The obligation of a kind of universality is laid upon theology by the character of the mythos itself—especially since in the Christian mythos we have to do with "God who created heaven and earth."[7] This means that theology cannot afford the luxury of the specialization which has so fragmented the University as to make its very name ironic. This, of course, does not mean that any one theologian must be competent in all fields of human inquiry, but rather that all need to be engaged in sympathetic and critical dialogue with other forms of inquiry and reflection. This may seem like rather a grandiose enterprise but it is in fact fundamental to the educational enterprise of the Christian community itself as it seeks to render accessible for all of its people the farthest and nearest ranges of human experience as these are illumined through the mythos.

A final aim of theological reflection is to facilitate the transformation of personal and social reality in obedience to the imperative character of the mythos. This may be termed *the practical or ethical task of theology.* Theology is not involved simply in the juggling or clarification of ideas—it drives toward practical implementation. It is concerned not simply with a way of knowing, but with a way of being, caring, and doing. Barth was one theologian who saw clearly that the disjunction of Christian theology from

Christian ethics was disastrous, and acted decisively to bring together in his *Church Dogmatics* what ought never to have been
separated. This ethical function of theology is being increasingly
emphasized by theologians such as Jürgen Moltmann and G.
Gutiérrez[8] and this is a development of major importance for the
future of theology. But it is not only with the transformation of
social reality that theology in its practical task has to deal. It is
also concerned with the transformation and healing of the lives of
persons. One of the most urgent tasks for theology at present is
the development of a genuinely pastoral theology which will decisively overcome the theological naivete of much pastoral care
and the oblivion to issues of human healing characteristic of much
theology. It is to the credit of Paul Tillich that he made some
significant steps in this direction[9]—steps which have not yet been
adequately explicated.

I have suggested four fundamental aims of theological reflection.
While it is possible to emphasize one or another of these functions,
it is clear that they really belong together. In pursuing these tasks
(which could be differently named and divided) theology, far from
obscuring or impoverishing the mythos, serves actually to facilitate
its own intention to represent, orient, communicate, and transform
existence in the world. In this way reflection and faith are joined.

THE PHENOMENOLOGICAL AND KERYGMATIC

We turn now to focus more directly upon a dialectic which has
tacitly informed our discussion thus far. There are two basic
directions in which theological reflection tends to move which may
be called the phenomenological and the kerygmatic. Phenomenological in this context designates that movement of reflection which
approaches theological categories from an analysis of the structure
of that which is given to human experience quite generally and
apart from the special claims of the mythos. It might also be
labeled inductive, empirical, philosophical, or natural theology.
Kerygmatic in this context designates the opposite direction of
reflection which moves from the mythos itself toward the development of theological categories with which to interpret experience.
It may also be labeled deductive, confessional, dogmatic, or
revelational.

These two directions of thought are capable of a number of
variations which in their plurality and mutual incompatibility

provide the context for very complex questions of epistemology. My intention here is not to deal with those issues in their intricacy, but rather to suggest a way of seeing the larger context of that discussion—a way which I trust will make possible some further perspective on the dialectical character of theological reflection. For this purpose, therefore, we shall content ourselves with lumping together a number of theological movements which display the general tendencies which will be labeled phenomenological and kerygmatic.

These two directions of thought are sometimes presented as antagonists embroiled in irreconcilable conflict. Thus in the early decades of this century, the supposition that one could gain important theological insight from an investigation of human experience, or through an inquiry into the general and fundamental structures of reality as these were accessible to common understanding or to philosophical (or scientific) reason, was attacked as a scurrilous substitution of human opinion for divine truth. Natural theology, as this offending movement was then known, was placed under unrelenting attack by the forces of kerygmatic theology represented most ably by Karl Barth. So vigorous was this dispute that the suggestion of Barth's friend and collaborator Brunner that a doctrine of creation might allow for some knowledge of God to be derived from a consideration of nature (human and otherwise) was greeted by a thunderbolt from Basel: *Nein*.[10]

Similarly, kerygmatic theology with its view that theology must generate its fundamental notions out of the mythos itself has been assailed for failing to take human experience wtih sufficient seriousness, displaying thereby an arrogant disregard for those to whom it addresses itself. It thus tends toward what Bonhoeffer termed a revelational positivism, in which theology drops its dicta upon an uncomprehending world like stones from heaven.

To a degree what is involved here is already anticipated in our discussion of faith and reflection, but it is important to give it some direct attention. This may best be done by examining each of the two fundamental directions of thought separately.

Phenomenological. The term phenomenological is used here in a very broad sense to designate a direction of thought shared by predominantly empirical, inductive, and even philosophical theologies. It refers to any procedure by which theological categories are derived from data or phenomena not themselves explicitly or specifically theological. Such a procedure usually involves heavy reliance upon prior philosophical or scientific analysis of that data and attempts to derive theological insights from the categories generated by that analysis.

This may be made more clear if we consider some typical examples of this sort of theological reflection.

What has come to be called existential theology is one example of the predominance of this direction in theological reflection. The philosophical analysis of Martin Heidegger has been most influential in the development of a very important contemporary theological style. Here the analysis of the structure of human existence (an analysis which is phenomenological in the stricter sense) produces a number of very important and suggestive concepts: authenticity, anxiety, decision, responsibility, the letting-be-of-being, and linguisticality. These provide an extensive vocabulary within which to bring the character of human existence to expression. The vocabulary thus produced may then be taken over into theological discussion to provide the meaning for an outmoded or worn out theological vocabulary (salvation, sin, faith, and providence).

A similar sort of movement occurs in process theology. Instead of proceeding from an analysis of the structure of human existence, the base of reflection here is provided by an analysis of the categories of a cosmology: causation, novelty, actual entity, relativity, and absolute. The analysis then is of the fundamental categories in terms of which it is possible to think of a world or universe. This analysis, most notably by Whitehead and then by Charles Hartshorne, generates a number of significant notions: the temporal character of all reality, the relativity of God to the world, the fundamental character of creativity, and the objective immortality of actual entities. These too provide an extensive vocabulary within which to articulate philosophical, scientific, and theological concerns. Some of these insights may then be used to interpret specifically theological concerns with respect to the nature of God, and the relation between God and the world. This has been done with particular distinction by John Cobb.

There are a large number of other theological currents which similarly employ this broadly phenomenological approach to theology. In general they generate their primary categories from some region of human experience—often psychological (especially humanistic or third force psychology) or sociological—and then make use of these categories to interpret theological concerns. This essay itself, though it is about rather than in theology, may be viewed as largely dominated by the phenomenological direction of thought.

All of these approaches share a common emphasis upon grounding theological discourse in an analysis of the experience of reality which gives this direction of thought its peculiarly phenomenological thrust.

This has the considerable merit of grounding theological discussion in an experience and understanding of reality accessible to Christian and non-Christian alike. It may thus serve as an appropriate procedure where the aim is fundamentally apologetic in character. It further serves to make clear that theology is not divorced in its concerns from other attempts to understand human existence and experience. It thus makes possible and encourages a lively and enlivening dialogue with other disciplines and alternative persuasions.

Despite these very great advantages, however, there is good reason to be wary of too excessive a claim for the merit of this approach. From quite early on in this essay it has been necessary to maintain that the access we have to reality and existence is one which is mediated by the imagination. There is no such thing as sheer induction where the pattern of intelligibility emerges directly from the phenomena without being simultaneously imposed upon the given phenomena in such a way as to transform them. Much of the attraction of a phenomenological approach to theology lies in the naive supposition that a purely objective and unmediated knowledge of reality is possible.

It is important to note here that the primarily phenomenological perspectives of Whitehead and Heidegger were themselves developed under the antecedent influence of the Christian mythos that they have subsequently been used to interpret. Thus the usefulness of such analyses of experience seems to depend, in part at least, upon a pre-understanding of the phenomenon itself partially determined by the Christian mythos. This in no way diminishes the value of such analyses nor that of the theologies which make major use of them. Instead it suggests that something rather like a kerygmatic movement of thought stands behind what otherwise appears as a phenomenological movement of thought. This can only be clarified if we turn now to a consideration of the kerygmatic in its own right.

Kerygmatic. The term kerygmatic stems from the Greek word for proclamation. Proclamation is the bringing to expression of that which comes to expression in the mythos. Thus it is a mode of speaking and, by extension, of understanding, which is fundamentally informed and controlled by the mythos. Here, in a movement of thought exactly opposite to what we have been calling the phenomenological, the principal categories of understanding are derived from the mythos itself and then used to interpret experience. Thus we may say that the categories of theological reflection are deduced from the mythos. It would also be appropriate to speak of this as a confessional approach to theologizing since it begins from the confession of faith determined by the mythos. Finally, since it intends to be controlled by and conformable to the mythos, it may, in a broad sense, be termed dogmatic. In the context of this discussion, therefore, these terms may be used interchangeably. A few examples of this movement may be helpful here.

There have been attempts to derive from the mythos fundamental insights which can then be employed to understand the nature of reality generally. Such procedures are frequently termed biblical metaphysics or Christian philosophy. But in order to move kerygmatically it is not necessary to do this across the board. Hegel, for example, derives from the Christian mythos two key elements: the incarnation of the Word and the eschatological direction of history. These two key notions provide a foundation on the basis of which to transform the idealistic philosophy of his day into a systematic philosophy of the progressive objectification of Absolute Spirit. While it may certainly be disputed whether the result is either biblical or specifically Christian, nevertheless two fundamental categories for constructing a way of viewing human history and activity are here borrowed from the Christian mythos.

Similarly, there have been a number of attempts to develop a working model of human society from the Christian mythos. Calvin in Geneva and the American Puritans are two of hundreds of such attempts. Again there is no need to do this in a comprehensive manner in order to demonstrate a kerygmatic movement of thought. So, for example, when Bonhoeffer called upon Christians in Germany to withstand the efforts to nationalize and centralize the church at the behest of Hitler, his position was derived from a theological judgment about the compatibility of Hitler's decrees with the necessity of the church to acknowledge Christ as sole Lord. So also Martin Luther King's call for justice and dignity for all people coupled with a stand for non-violence was derived, at least in part, from a consideration of the implications of Christian faith for a given social circumstance.

Other kinds of examples could be multiplied indefinitely. What is crucial here is the direction in which theological reflection moves. It is not that a kerygmatic or dogmatic mode of reflection ignores human reality, but that it approaches it from the point of view of the mythos.

The examples which have been cited suggest, however, that this kerygmatic movement of reflection does not function without some admixture of a phenomenological direction of thought. The questions addressed to the mythos, political, philosophical, and psychological, help to determine the sort of fundamental concepts which are derived from it. But these questions seem themselves to be derived from a prior participation in some region of human experience not itself directly or immediately within the language of the mythos. The question regarding a biblical concept of justice itself is informed by the way in which the issue of justice has become a crucial one for the theologian. Thus the question itself seems to derive from a pre-understanding of a phenomenological sort. It would appear that the derivation of theological categories from the mythos by way of deduction itself seems to presuppose a phenomenological direction of thought, giving rise to the questions which determine what sort of categories are to be sought.

At this point then, it seems that, far from being enemies, the phenomenological and kerygmatic directions of thought require one another. Indeed, if we consider what might be the result of their separation from one another we may see more clearly why this must be so. It is possible to develop a suspicion of the kerygmatic movement of thought—claiming that it cuts off dialogue with the world. Thus one may seek to maximize and purify the phenomenological approach to theology claiming that thereby one is likely to maximize the opportunity for dialogue with other disciplines and achieve a view of reality more in keeping with the way in which people actually experience themselves and their world.

Such an attempt must, however, be ultimately self-defeating. In the first place, much of its persuasiveness derives from the lingering supposition that a view of reality independent of prior images of

reality is possible. This has rootage in the ideology of objectivity.
A kind of gullibility or superstition then facilitates the naive appropriation of philosophical or scientific or other notions which the
theologian is in no position to evaluate.

Perhaps more serious, however, is a second liability which a
phenomenological approach to theology may accept. To the extent
that conceptuality or language appropriated from other disciplines
or worlds of discourse come to dominate theological discussion,
then theology may itself increasingly be reduced to an echo. In
this case theology forfeits its responsibility to make a genuine contribution to the dialogue. Instead it simply supplies a veneer of
religious language within which to say what is already being said.

This is what some critics have supposed to be taking place in
Bultmann's existential interpretation. Should it be the case that
the categories derived from an analysis of human existence so completely interpret the mythos as to leave it without uninterpreted
remainder, then the mythos has become an arcane allegory for an
adequate understanding of existence. The mythos once interpreted
would then be superfluous. In that case what began as a dialogue
between existential and biblical perspectives has become a monologue. There are important ways in which Bultmann keeps this
from happening and it is precisely by way of a kergymatic direction
of thought that such a limit is introduced.

The situation is far more serious in areas less subject to direct
exegetical discussion than New Testament scholarship. Much of
what passes for a discussion between theology and sociology, or
especially theology and psychology, can be readily seen to be a
monologue in which the only function of theology is to provide an
arcane and vaguely Christian translation of an otherwise secular
theory and practice. The result is usually the reduction of psychology or sociology to catch-phrases and the elimination altogether of
theological insight. The equation of actualizing human potential
with justification and reconciliation, for example, contributes nothing to psychological or theological insight, and in fact so obscures
the issues as to stop any thinking process dead in its tracks. If
what is today called meaningful dialogue is to take place then it can
do so only if theology brings its own perspective to bear upon such
issues. The way in which such a perspective arises, however, is
by way of a movement *from* the mythos toward psychological or
sociological inquiry. This is what has been called here the kerygmatic direction of theological reflection.

It was this kind of reduction of theological discourse brought on by the ascendancy of a phenomenological direction in theology which, in a different context, caused the reaction of neo-orthodox theology in the early part of this century. But the attempt to purify theology of a phenomenological movement of thought in the interest of a more fully kerygmatic movement is equally self-stultifying.

First, as already noted, it fails to notice the way in which the very questions in terms of which the mythos is elaborated are themselves derived from the situation of the interpreter and are cast into the language of a contemporary sensibility. This means that a purely kerygmatic direction is impossible.

To the extent, however, that a theology depends heavily upon the kerygmatic direction, it runs the risk of becoming anachronistic or narrow. It becomes anachronistic when it simply reiterates previous formulations attempting to ignore contemporary issues, questions, and language (if these are taken into account then a phenomenological movement is introduced). It becomes narrow when it delimits the sphere of theological issues in such a way as to isolate them from the baleful influence of philosophy, science, or the Zeitgeist. In either case such a theology becomes a linguistic ghetto.[11] But by its very nature of being responsive to the Christian mythos, theology ceases to exist under these circumstances. Our discussion of the temporal character of the mythos indicates that it is violated by an anachronistic, purely past-oriented interpretation. Any attempt to restrict theology to sectarian interests is a similar violation of the character of a mythos which functions to knit together all dimensions of reality by virtue of the presence of the sacred.

It would be more precise to say that the relationship between these two directions is dialectical. By that I mean that the two directions are in genuine tension with one another while still requiring one another. An attempt to do theology in only one of these directions must either prove itself abortive or disguise its actual dependence upon the contrary direction of reflection. The movement back and forth in these two directions gives to theology its characteristic structure.

In a broader context this structure has been termed the hermeneutical circle or spiral. This terminology suggests the way in which meaning emerges from the complex and thus never one-directional relationship between the subject and the object of inter-

pretation. In theology the movement from experience to mythos
to experience has the character of a lively discussion into which one
enters without being able to say who it is in the discussion that
has had the first word or will have the last. In any particular
theological investigation one is involved in the dynamic of this
movement often without being able to say whether it began induc-
tively or deductively. The task in such a situation, then, is to
attempt to discover some, perhaps previously unnoticed, range of
agreement in which both directions of thought are able to make a
substantial contribution to the position of the other.

This is not to say that one finds an ultimate coincidence of these
contrary movements of thought. That would be a transcendence
or avoidance of the tension constitutive of theological reflection.
To assert a dialectical relationship between these two directions
then is not to posit a grand Hegelian synthesis but to draw attention to the permanently dialectical character of theological reflection.

What I am contending for here is a maximizing of both directions
of thought as the course most likely to generate a theological understanding which is most adequate to the mythos *and* to contemporary experiencing of reality. A theology which does not directly
engage the lived experience of our world effectively stifles the
functioning of the mythos. A theology, however, which simply
echoes the commonplaces of that experience without effectively
challenging them is not worth anyone's trouble to read or write
or seriously entertain. It seems that it is the latter by which
American students and teachers of theology are the most readily
tempted. If that is true then the American context calls for a
renewed emphasis upon the kerygmatic direction of theological
reflection.

In any case the dialectical character of theological reflection is
not limited to the relationship between the phenomenological or
inductive and kerygmatic or deductive directions of reflection. We
have already seen how faith and reflection constitute a similar
irreducible yet intimately united polarity. This emphasis upon
polarities which are irreducible yet bound together determines the
structure of the subsequent discussion of theological method.

NOTES

1. Michael Polanyi, *Personal Knowledge* (Chicago: University of
Chicago Press, 1959) and Thomas Kuhn, *The Structures of Scientific
Revolutions* (Chicago: University of Chicago Press, 1962).

2. Cf. *New Essays in Philosophical Theology*, ed. Anthony Flew and Alasdair MacIntyre (London: SCM Press, 1955), p. 100.

3. A helpful discussion of this issue may be found in Frederic Ferré, *Language, Logic and God* (New York: Harper and Row, 1961).

4. A different and also helpful ordering of the primary theological tasks may be found in Bernard Lonergan, *Method in Theology* (New York: Herder & Herder, 1972).

5. Eberhard Bethge, *Dietrich Bonhoeffer* (New York: Harper & Row, 1970), pp. 298 ff.

6. Paul Tillich, *Systematic Theology*, I, pp. 59 ff.

7. Wolfhart Pannenberg, *The Apostles' Creed*, trans. Margaret Kohl (Philadelphia: Westminster Press, 1972), p. 34.

8. Gustavo Gutiérrez, *A Theology of Liberation*, trans. C. Inda and J. Eagleson (Maryknoll: Orbis, 1973).

9. Tillich prosecutes this "pastoral" task more notably in his *The Courage To Be* (New Haven: Yale University Press, 1952) and in his various collections of sermons.

10. *Natural Theology* (comprising "Nature and Grace" by Prof. Dr. Emil Brunner and the reply "No" by Dr. Karl Barth), trans. Peter Frankel and Introduction by John Baillie (London: Bles, 1946).

11. The concern to liberate theology from such a ghetto is one which I share with my teacher and friend Hendrick Boers whose book *Theology Out of the Ghetto* (Leiden: E. J. Brill, 1971) is an attempt to uncover the exegetical foundations of such a task.

Chapter 7

Past and Present

The polarity of past and present is determinative of the character of theology's reflective process. In a period of virtually unrelieved contemporaneity the preoccupation of theology with its own past may make it seem something of an anachronism. The task of this chapter is to explore some of the ways in which theology's adverting to the past gives it its peculiar prius upon the present, within which and on behalf of which its reflections move.

The question of its proper relationship to past and present has been particularly troublesome for theology in the modern period. Van Harvey describes recent theology as a "series of salvage operations"[1] that have sought to rescue whatever possible from the collapse of a relationship between past and present, which, until the modern period, functioned to mediate this dialogue between past and present almost effortlessly. It is indeed only in the period of modern (post-enlightenment) theology that the question of the relationship of theological reflection to the past and thus its historical character became sufficiently acute to be formulated in any clear way.

The relationship of theological reflection to the past must in any case be distinguished from a nostalgia for a golden age (though there are echoes of nostalgia in some references to the earliest Christian communities) or an archivalist sentiment which prizes antiquity for its own sake. *The concern of theology is rather with a past that founds the present and drives it (or lures it) toward the future.* It is the amplification of the meaning of that thesis to which this chapter will be devoted.

The path taken to establish that thesis will be, however, a circuitous one. After some provisional reflections upon the nature of the authority of the past for religious imagination generally and in the Christian mythos particularly, it will be necessary to inquire

108

into the significance of the scripture and tradition dichotomy in order to gain a bearing upon the way in which the problem of theology's relation to the past has been usually brought into focus. That discussion will then lead to the question of interpretation and thence to the question of the significance of this dialectic of interpretation for an understanding of human life. The last section will therefore attempt to make clear in what way the dialectic of past and present may be recognized as determinative, not only of theological discourse, but of human experience generally.

THE MYTHOS AND THE PAST

The products of the religious imagination typically refer to a point in time which has since receded into the past. Particularly in the case of myth and ritual (though less clearly in the case of vision) the reference is to a prior and usually primordial time. We have noted previously the tendency of a mythos to refer to the time of origin and thus to the beginning of time. In this way the regions of experience derive their significance from their original foundation. Subsequent hierophanies seem to be assimilated to this primordial time which is made contemporary through the telling and hearing of the mythic narrative or the enacting of the ritual. A fundamental structure of the religious imagination, therefore, seems to be the interrelation of time past (and primordial) to time present in such a way as to place the present under the protective signification of the past. That is, the meaning of present existence is guaranteed through participation (via myth and ritual) in the primordial or strong time.

The reference to the past, especially to a primordial or anonymous past, does not yet produce history and thus is not a reference to the past in the sense to which we have become accustomed. Doubtless it would be possible to introduce a number of qualifying characteristics which could be adduced to distinguish more precisely the specific form of any religious community's reference to the past. Our concern here is to indicate the way in which the above structure is modified for the Christian mythos in such a way as to contribute to what we would today begin to recognize as history.

In the Christian mythos, the reference is no longer to an anonymous past but to a particular past whose antecedents and successors are thereby brought into sharp relief (in part through our

habit of counting years in both directions—A. D. and B. C. from
the calculated [or miscalculated] year of Jesus' birth). Now we
have already had occasion to examine some of the consequences
of this reference to a particular and therefore no longer anonymous
or primordial past in a previous chapter,[2] and these need not be
repeated at length here. It need only be reiterated that the reference to a concrete past is wed to the insistence upon the reality
of the temporal, and thus of history as the locus of meaning.

The horizon of meaning thereby established induces a consciousness of history and thus makes necessary a dialectic which moves
between past and present in the quest of understanding. This
occurs by way of a second and related feature of the mythos,
namely, that it receives crucial and early formulation in a set of
texts and, in addition, that the subsequent interpretations and
elaborations of that mythos are also committed to writing. In a
society in which a mythos is transmitted orally without recourse
to a text, there is no possibility of noting a discrepancy or variation in the mythos from one generation to the next. The absence
of the possibility of a disjunction between past and present, and
therefore the absence of a consciousness of history, is directly
related to the absence of a crucial role being played by a text. But
in Christianity, as in Judaism before and Islam after, a collection
of texts is made the primary locus of the mythos. We will explore
some of the ramifications of this later under the rubrics of Scripture and tradition and hermeneutics but here my primary point is
to suggest the way in which the question of a relation to the past
arises for Christian theology.

Since it is the character of a mythos generally, and of the Christian mythos particularly, to establish a horizon of meaning within
which a community lives, it entails a reference not only to the past
but to the present as well. Thus, in the case of the Christian
mythos the reference of the mythos to a particular past and the
designation of a set of texts as primary locus of the mythos cannot
be allowed to obscure the functioning of the mythos as a conveyor
of present (contemporary) meaning. The attempt to apply received meanings to present circumstances, or to reformulate those
meanings within an altered context of meaning is the problem of
interpretation with which theology is necessarily involved.

Theological reflection then entails a movement between past
and present which, to a large degree, corresponds to the polar

directions of reflection which I have termed phenomenological and dogmatic. The dogmatic direction of reflection is one which attempts to gain leverage upon the present by way of recourse to received symbols. If that is done in such a way as to impose the structure of meaning received from the past upon the present in a heteronomous fashion, then the term dogmatic receives and deserves a pejorative connotation. The phenomenological direction of reflection attempts to gain leverage upon the meaning of received symbols by way of an analysis or present experience. If that proceeds in such a way as to silence those symbols then the phenomenological reduction becomes, in the pejorative sense, reductionistic.

THE AUTHORITY OF THE PAST

The question of the authority of the past is therefore crucial to theology. Upon the possibility of reaching some clarity on that question hinges the possibility of a viable theological enterprise. It may be useful therefore to note some of the more important ways in which that question has been addressed, not so much in order to find a response which we may embrace as to illustrate the nature of the problem. This will then put us in the position of attempting a more fruitful formulation of the question of the authority of the past. Since such questions typically focus upon the authority of scripture and authority of tradition, these will be briefly reviewed here.

For the first few centuries of its existence the Christian community managed to get along rather well without a formal canon of its own. In the patristic period, writings of early Christian leaders, together with the writings of the Old Testament, functioned as normative in varying degrees. There was considerable variation among communities as to the selection of documents which thus functioned. Only under the impetus provided by Marcion, and in reaction to his elimination of many texts which had assumed great importance in a large number of Christian communities, did the church commence serious deliberation upon the question of which documents could be taken to be authoritative.[3]

Authority in this case was closely associated with apostolicity of authorship; that is, the question of which of the documents were written by or under the immediate influence of the first leaders of the community. The intention lying behind such a criterion seems to be that of safeguarding it against the wholesale importation of syncretistic elements which would jeopardize the community's identity amidst the swarm of mystery cults and gnostic speculations which engulfed the Hellenistic world. The documents thus singled out were taken to be reliable witnesses to the fundamental structure of the faith. In practice a second criterion, less explicit, was also at work in the process of selection—namely, the inclusion of documents whose authorship was greatly disputed but which did serve in a number of communities as important parts of their liturgical and theological canon (thus *Hebrews*, for example). As noted previously, a mythos functions for and within a community. Therefore is was altogether appropriate that elements taken to be normative expressions of that mythos within a community could find a place in the canonical or normative collection. The appropriateness of reaching a judgment about this by political means should also be apparent.

The collection thus formed served as a charter or constitution for the community.[4] Acknowledgment of its teaching, its moral precepts, the view of world and God and humanity which it contained, secured the identity of the community. It could serve therefore as a guidebook for doctrine and moral order. More than that, however, it presented the paradigmatic account of the story of the community. Naturally the Bible was in practice supplemented by various other sources of guidance: the customs of the communities, the teaching of figures of major importance such as bishops and theologians (for several centuries most theologians were bishops—though even then the converse did not hold—in any case the combination has become increasingly rare and now verges upon extinction).

The practice of the community came to be the establishment of correct interpretation by reference to a variety of validating sources: the Bible, the decisions of councils of bishops, the writings of particularly prestigious earlier theologians, and custom sanctioned hierarchically. So long as interpretation, especially of Scripture, was permitted to move on several planes other than a common-sense reading (what was called literal then—a word which is too misleading in the modern period), there was little difficulty in supposing that these sources constituted a seamless web of meaning. In principle Scripture was still taken to be fundamental, but since in practice no real contradiction seemed to arise (only specialists handled the documents anyway) the other sources could be appealed to as well, and indeed in such a way as to place them on an equal and often superior footing.

This interpretive famework already began to show signs of wear and tear by the time of the High Middle Ages, but was not effectively challenged until the time of Martin Luther. It was Luther's contention that a vast number of doctrines, practices, and institutions had grown up under this umbrella which fundamentally obscured and, indeed, perverted the community and its faith. The only way to cut through to what was authentically of the essence of faith was by way of a turn toward the single and undiluted authority of the Bible. Thus the watchword: *sola scriptura*. Luther's position was not intended to deny the importance of the early councils or the writings of early theologians. But he did want to deny that there was any expression of Christian faith which stood on equal footing with Scripture, and that whatever could not be shown to be clearly consistent with it must be discarded. To the objection that, without the exercise of the teaching office of the community as manifest in the institutional structures then prevailing, Scripture was obscure, Luther replied with the doctrine of the clarity (*claritas*) of Scripture. What this meant was that a straightforward interpretation of Scripture was possible (Scripture is not obscure) and that only such an interpretation was permissible.

Luther was more keenly aware than many of his followers or colleagues (Calvin, for example) that there were conflicting perspectives in the texts of the New Testament. This was, for example, clearly the case with respect to Paul and James on the question of justification. But he was confident that the principle of interpreting Scripture (and thus for deciding between rival perspectives within Scripture) was itself given in the New Testament. Stated briefly, the authority of Scripture is measured in accordance with its ability to "bear Christ." That which attests to and makes actual the significance of Christ is alone authoritative for the Christian.

This introduces a rather different conception of authority. The Bible is not regarded as authoritative in the way in which a legal document is. Instead its authority is understood as an *activity,* namely, that of bearing and making manifest that to which it attests. The view which I put forward earlier about the way in which one recognizes oneself and one's world in the mythos is a distant descendant of the actualism[5] of Luther's view of authority.

Luther's rather complex view of the authority of Scripture was swiftly replaced in the period of Protestant orthodoxy (or Protestant scholasticism) by what is known today as biblicism. Its emergence derives in part from Calvin's view of Scripture which had no place for Luther's actualism but posited a blanket authority for the Bible. Far more rigidly than Luther had ever done the Bible was made to be the constitution of the community. Growing up around this view and supporting it was the notion of the verbal (or literal) inspiration of the text. In part this thesis was fashioned to counteract Catholic claims that the church was the author (at least proximately) of the text and therefore its proper interpreter. But the development of the view in the seventeenth century and beyond is also related to the peculiary modern quest for an absolute immanent authority. Many candidates have been offered for this position, among them reason, sense-experience, the state, the pope, and the "principle of verifiability." Biblicism offers Scripture as its candidate in this dubious sweepstakes.

The notion of authority is thus fatefully (and as the grim history of this century also shows, fatally) altered. It no longer means that in terms of which a community recognizes and understands itself, nor does it mean that which conveys the revelatory foundation of the community to the community. It is now an iron decree itself identical with absolute truth. The biblical name for such an immanent absolute is idolatry—it is, as we have learned to our sorrow, an all consuming Moloch. Even to those who know better, the very word authority has the ring of authoritarian.

So, at least, it appears from the vantage of hindsight. At the time it must have seemed crucial to have a clear defense against a chaotic proliferation of interpretations and authorities. The existence of the community required a defining principle which could not be eroded by doubt and disputation. We live by meanings and the defense of meaning may, in the face of a chaotic swirl of conflicting opinion, seem to require the designation of something as indubitable. Such views do not arise at all with the intent to coerce adherence but, by the inner logic of the quest for certainty, they must resolutely suppress rivals and thus become coercive.

Two views emerged to compete with the biblicist perspective and they may be designated as modernism and pietism. The modernist view adopted the understanding of the Bible as an objective and literally intended text which could be viewed as being a doctrinal and ethical handbook. Stemming from Luther's view of the *claritas* of Scripture it sought to understand the text in the way in which the text was orignially understood by way of an investigation of the history and situation of the text. Thus was launched the scientific investigation of the meaning of biblical texts. Unilke the biblicism from which it in part descended, however, modernism subjects the authority of the text to the authority of rational inquiry. Thus the authority of the text derives its validation through critical inquiry. Authority is attributed to, rather than contributed by, the text.

In contrast to the objectivism which characterizes the biblicist and modernist understanding of the authority of the text, pietism makes much of the internal witness of the Spirit in the heart of the believer. The biblicist had in the Bible the indubitable and dictated word and will of God. The modernist had found in it universal moral truths. Both, to the pietist, had simply the dead letter. The text has no authority in and of itself. Authority derives from the Spirit alone. Despite the fact that this position represents the actualist side of Luther's position and its healthy suspicion of the tendencies to objectify the Bible in biblicism and modernism, the pietist account of the authority of Scripture tends to cut the nerve of the function of such texts to found a community. The subjectivism tends to become an individualism (something not unknown to the modernist) and at its extreme to substitute a private and incommunicable experience for the shared meanings of the mythos. Thus the possibility of reliable and discussable interpretation is vitiated. The arid intellectualism of the modernist and biblicist approach is rejected by pietism but only to be replaced with what must ultimately become silence.

This historico-critical investigation of Scripture, which engendered and was nourished by modernism together with a somewhat modified form of pietism, gives rise to the dominant forms of twentieth century responses to the question of the authority of the Bible. The principle of *sola scriptura* which governed the Protestant views we have been looking at receives an added and altered significance influenced by the recovery of Luther's perspective abetted by the Luther Renaissance at the beginning of this century. The texts are no longer regarded as objective in the sense of a constitution or charter but as the bearer of faith. The principle of the clarity of Scripture is generally replaced or modified by historico-critical investigation. Frequently, though not always, Luther's criterion of "that which bears Christ" is modified to "that which communicates authentic existence." In any case the Bible is not regarded as a handbook of reasonable or revealed moral and doctrinal precepts but as proclamation which evokes faith. In this view the authority of the Bible is not something which it has *ex officio*, nor something which an autonomous reason may attribute to it, but is something more like an event. Authority "happens" between the text and the hearer. Subjectivism is guarded against by an appeal to historico-critical inquiry (e.g., Bultmann) or an appeal to the community persisting through time as hearer of the word (Barth).

Now these rather rough and ready characterizations should not be taken as an attempt at history. The various positions to which I have referred are far more complex than it would be possible or appropriate to suggest in an essay of this type. My main intent is to get clear what is at stake in the question of the authority of Scripture and, by extension, the authority of the mythos as it is received from the past.

The question of authority need not be formulated in such a way as to produce a response which is authoritarian in nature (just as one may do dogmatic theology without lapsing into dogmatism, or be a scientist without embracing scientism). Any formulation of authority which verges upon a heteronomous imposition of the mythos or some portion of it, clearly violates the character of a mythos by literalizing and objectivizing it. A formulation which makes its meaning incommunicable, or which ignores its function of identifying and founding a community, entails a similar violation of the nature of a mythos.

More positively we may say that the authority of Scripture should be conceived in such a way as to take into account: a) its character as a product of the religious imagination (i.e., its character as embracing myth, symbol, and apocalyptic); b) its communal character (its limits fixed by the community, its images forming and informing the continuing life of that community); c) its character as not only describing that to which it points but actually conveying it. Of course, this does not constitute a formal answer to the question of the authority of the Bible. It does, however, attempt to point in the direction in which responsible positions may lie. Most of all, I want to make clear that literalism, absolutism, and individualism do not give adequate responses to the issue.

We must formulate a response to the question of authority in such a way as to absolutize neither the text nor the interpreter. This can be done only by focusing upon how it is that any text or image or discourse has its authority. If we notice carefully how this happens then several features begin to emerge clearly. First, when we recognize our world and existence as decisively illumined by a text (take, for example, a poem of T. S. Eliot) then we may properly say that that text speaks to us with authority. In this case the text is not imposed upon us from the outside or arbitrarily. But neither are we the authors of the text and its authority. By it we have been addressed in a way in which we could not address ourselves. The more fundamental and comprehensive the illumination, the greater the degree of authority. If to this is added the inseparability of the meaning from the text, then its authority persists. If the text is an allegory, or the statement of a general and variously accessible truth, then the text becomes dispensable once we have mastered the point of the text (though we still remain indebted to it). In the case of more radically symbolical or mythic texts where a reduction of the text by reflection to its point is blocked by the density and multiplicty and particularities of its signification, it remains, as I have suggested before, the irreplaceable ground of reflection. Thus a new dimension of authority is added. Moreover, when this text constitutes the ground of self-understanding for the community within which we have our life, and thus serves as the basis for the sharing of existence within that community, a further dimension of authority comes into view. Finally, we may add to this the power of the symbol, not only to represent, but also to communicate its given. When this given is recognized as the grounding of existence in the life and meaning giving power of the sacred, then a final dimension of authority appears.

Now I am not maintaining that this happens all at once. Nor is it necessary to posit all of these dimensions in order to speak meaningfully of authority. In no case does authority become absolute in such a way as to become altogether independent of the recognition of the hearer or community of hearers. The past has authority to the degree that it is recognized as the source and foundation of contemporary meaning.

SCRIPTURE AND TRADITION

The basic formulation of the problem of Scripture and tradition is to be found in the decisions of the Council of Trent. The position formulated there against that of the reformers is that it is untenable to restrict the normative expression of the mythos to Scripture, but that this must be expanded to include non-written (oral) tradition which stems from the apostles and is faithfully transmitted in the church through its teaching office. As a result of a long line of development, the papal office is ultimately designated as the normative bearer and articulator of this oral tradition. This position opens the way for the warranting of practice and doctrine through appeal to an authority of equal rank with Scripture (though not in contradiction to it).

The difficulty (and corresponding advantage) of such a position is that it allows of no real check against the intrusion of alien elements which may distort the life and understanding of the community. Authenticity is secured by appeal to the infallible guidance of the Spirit, especially as institutionalized (implicitly before but explicitly only in the last century) in the papal office. In any case this position allows for the warranting of institutions, liturgical practice, moral guidance, and doctrine not explicitly warranted in Scripture, thus providing for a process of adaptation of the community without the need for a revision of its constitutional documents.

The position is generally rejected by Protestant theologians on the grounds that it delivers the given of theological discourse as well as its content into the hands of the human (and therefore fallible) institutions of the church. The church thus becomes, in practice if not in theory, the source of revelation.

The Catholic position[6] may point out for its side, first, that the documents of the New Testament are themselves the product of the community which reduced to writing some (though not all) of the authentic teaching of the earliest Christian leaders.

Second, the reduction of the mythos to Scripture necessarily produces both biblicism and individualism, thereby dividing the community into endlessly proliferating sects. What is needed, and what Protestantism cannot provide, is a clear test of the validity of an interpretation of Scripture. The absence of such a test produces individualism and sectarianism. What better way to introduce appropriate guidance in these matters than by way of appeal to the living presence of the apostolic faith in the community as a whole and made visible in its responsible leadership?

Finally, biblicism produced by the Protestant approach event- uates in the dismissal of the whole of the history of the community. It is, despite its pretentions to the contrary, utterly a-historical. Biblicism is a kind of chauvinism of the present which dismisses all time intervening between it and the paradigmatic past as irrelevant at best and fundamental distortion at worst.

Now it seems to me that it is possible to answer these objections without falling into the liabilities so often associated with the Protestant position. The basis for such a response is grounded in the perspective provided by a consideration of the nature of a mythos generally and the Christian mythos particularly.

We must note first, with respect to the mythos, that it is indeed produced by the community. This is true in a twofold way. The writings, rituals, and images which function as a part of the mythos do spring from the faith of the community. They are the ways in which the community gives expression to that event by which it is founded. Moreover, the community determines which of these expressions most adequately represent its faith. It cannot be said, however, that the community is sovereign over what it has thus produced and recognized. The establishment of the canon of Scripture, for example, is the response of the community to documents whose authority transcends that of the community. In them the community recognizes itself, that is, acknowledges that these documents truly express the reality of that community in the world. The authority of the documents then does not *derive* from the community but is acknowledged by the community. This is so since the documents give expression to that event which founds the community and thus transcends it. The community therefore does not produce revelation but acknowledges that revelation is given authoritative and reliable expression in just these documents. In this way it is possible to acknowledge the decisive place of the community without making it the author of itself.

It is possible to agree fully with the assertion that theology cannot proceed in the historical vacuum of an isolated past (sedimented into the Bible) and an isolated present. Theology which ignores altogether the intervening history of church and theology consigns itself to imprisonment in the thought pattern of its own day and isolates itself from the community of faith and of theology.

Theology does not begin—it continues. When we do theology we insert ourselves into a conversation which has been proceeding, sometimes in lively, sometimes in desultory, fashion for two thousand years. If we jump in without having listened in on some of that dialogue, the chances are good that we will have missed some important points, and that what we say may be beside the point altogether. This is all the more so if we accept Gerhard Ebeling's suggestion and regard the history of theology as the history of biblical interpretation.[7] If the task of theology is that of explicating and applying the mythos to the present context, then we are likely to gain considerable aid from understanding how that task was prosecuted before us. If nothing else, we may learn to our profit that all formulations of the meaning of the mythos are provisional. But we are likely to learn much more as we observe the elaboration and articulation of the mythos into new and productive images and insights.

But still more needs to be said here. An explication of the mythos which evades its historical and communal power, as attested by the history of community and theology, is faulty from the standpoint of the mythos itself. I have emphasized that the mythos locates meaning in history. Meaning is not separable from its historical fate. The responses which it evokes in the fifth or thirteenth or nineteenth centuries are a part of its meaning, for it is not a bundle of timeless truths dropped from heaven like a stone, but the product and creator of history. Insofar as we recognize ourselves in this mythos, we shall be led to inquire into the history it has shaped and which shapes us. Thus the critical history of theology is itself not only a purely historical task but a necsesary theological task as well, as Karl Barth has rightly maintained.[8]

Finally, we must not only admit but also insist that there is a sense in which the oral takes precedence over the written. This Luther clearly saw, as his followers did not, and this provides a fundamental point of possible contact between the Protestant and Catholic positions.[9] The priority of the oral over the written may be seen in several ways. First, it is the character of myth to be told —that is, it is a narrative. Its reduction to writing is almost always secondary. Second, we may note that the Christian mythos takes the primary form of proclamation—a message spoken to a hearer. The writings of the New Testament are secondary formulations of this proclamation (so in the case of Paul who regularly laments the distance which makes recourse to writing necessary). Finally, the Christian mythos not only arises from but drives toward proclamation. This last is a matter which will be given preliminary treatment at the end of this essay, but which properly belongs to a doctrine of the Word of God and thus falls outside the limits of our task here.

But to concede all of this to the position of Scripture *and* tradition is not to give up the principle of *sola scriptura*. The exclusive particle (*sola*) does not entail the elimination of or solicit oblivion to other ingredients of the mythos and its elaboration. Instead it is a way of properly insisting upon the essential pastness and thus determinateness of the mythos. The temptation present in the "and" of Scripture and tradition is to dissolve the particularity of the past into the illusion of contemporaneity. The distance between past and present is thus prematurely abrogated, leaving us in the essentially timeless state of an enduring present. The discreteness of the canon mirrors the discreteness of the particular past we sometimes call the Christ-event. It is this particularity which gives identity to the community and summons the full and necessary elaboration of tradition (theological, liturgical, institutional) to integrity. This is not to say that integrity is thereby guaranteed. It is clearly not—otherwise one would hear no talk of continuing reformation. Nor is it to be construed as a summons to repristination. Theology lives out of the past but not in it. That too is a consequence of the reality of time. I am therefore maintaining that Scripture occupies a singularly normative position within the mythos which ought not to be violated by the promiscuous "and."

But is this position regarding the singularly normative status of Scripture in the mythos congruent with the position sketched earlier with respect to authority? An affirmative reply may be made on the following grounds. Both Protestant and Catholic affirm the authority of Scripture. Both are in agreement in recognizing the authority of the mythos which comes to expression in and outside of Scripture. The issue is in what way is the discreteness, the determinateness of that mythos best safeguarded (without determinateness no recognition, hence no authority and also no identifiable meaning). Is that discreteness more adequately mirrored in the teaching office of the church derived from oral tradition and located ultimately in *ex cathedra* pronouncements; or in the canonical documents in which the mythos receives expression, whose reliability is acknowledged by both Protestant and Catholic, and which, like the event to which they testify, is located in a particular past?   If the latter position is adopted it renders all the more crucial the question of hermeneutics to which I will next turn.

HERMENEUTICS

The preceding discussion opens up upon the question of hermeneutics.   It concluded with an insistence upon the salutary character of a certain distance between past and present which forces interpretation to take account of the sheer pastness of the past, thereby giving interpretive reflection a determinate object.   But this renders acute the question of the way in which the meanings of a past text may be carried forward into the present.   If this move is impossible then preoccupation with the texts becomes the province of the archivalist and museum keeper and not the theologian.   The question to which hermeneutics responds is in what way may the meaning of a text be made contemporary?

Obviously the question has great urgency for theology, especially Protestant theology with its emphasis upon the significance of an ancient text for contemporary existence.   It is in the context of post-Reformation theology that the question of hermeneutic (the theory and principles of interpretation) is first made the theme of a full-length treatment.[10]   The question, however, is also especially apparent for the study of law and also of literature generally.   The Enlightenment witnessed the emergence of a number of discussions of the heremeneutics appropriate to each discipline.   The attempt to unify all theories governing interpretation into a single theory of interpretation as such, was inaugurated by Friedrich Schleiermacher and has been continued by such philosophers as Dilthey, Heidegger, and Hans-Georg Gadamer.[11]   Rather than approach the question of a general hermeneutic, I will restrict my attention here to a discussion of the way in which the theory of the interpretation of a text holds a crucial place in theological reflection, and to sketch some of the conditions which any such theory must fulfill if it is to adequately describe the activity of interpretation appropriate to theology.

Between the past and the present, Lessing noted, the nascent historical criticism of the Enlightenment had opened a "deep ugly ditch."   With the advance of historico-critical methods the ditch has widened to become a gaping chasm. The advance of historical criticism has been spurred by the determination to loosen the documents of the past from the dogmatic assumptions of the present—attempting to understand them in terms of their own context and life-situation, however alien that may be to our own. Much of the impetus for historical criticism has been supplied by Luther's dictum of the clarity of Scripture, which entailed that these documents should be understood from themselves rather than by means of an intepretative framework supplied by tradition. The consequence of this release of the text from conformity with the world view of the interpreter has been the growing awareness of the distance between ancient and modern perspectives—a distance which increasingly has threatened to swallow the interpretive bridges hastily thrown across the widening gulf.

If the locus of meaning is assigned to the past and the documents which derive from an ancient world view, then one may be driven either to deny the chasm between past and present, or to designate its breadth as the measure by which the present has fallen away from truth (i.e., sin). The means by which these positions (often held together: the gap exists for you on account of your sin but not for me. . .) are defended and explicated, however, render them implausible. A defense of such a position often entails the reduction of the texts (in this case, biblical texts) to literal propositions. That this does violence to the sort of texts they are (i.e., products of the religious imagination) is clear from our previous discussion of the character of such texts. But it should also be noted that a literalizing of the text is also a peculiarly modern phenomenon. It depends in part for its plausibility upon the fixing of the text in widely distributed (printed) editions.[12] Far more, however, it depends upon the peculiarly modern sense of literal truth, itself a perspective far removed from the texts themselves with their clear evidence of the free adaptation (never repetition) of antecedent materials (oral and written). Thus the literal repetition of past meanings turns out to be a peculiarly modern interpretation of them. In the meantime, however, the present is evaded on another front, setting up the multiple conflicts between science and religion so much a part of our recent past. Such conflicts tend to foster confidence on the part of the religionists that they have successfully prosecuted their aim of re-presenting the past meanings in an age which, by hypothesis, has fallen away from truth. Far more importantly, however, they set up unwarranted conflicts in perception which deny to the mythos its function of authentically interpreting present experience. The mythos is thus rendered ineffective by the very attempt to preserve or conserve its meanings.

A second option may be to place meaning in the present. This after all is where the interpreter necessarily stands, and it is in this space that the word of meaning must resound if it is to resound at all. The most extreme way of locating meaning in the present may be represented by Chesterton's characterization of the nineteenth century historiographers who believed that history was a story which had a good ending because it ended with them. With respect to the interpretation of Scripture this position simply presents the thesis that what was formerly hid in darkness may now be made manifest thanks to the wonders of modern scientific scholarship. To a certain degree, of course, we all share this presupposition, though we may blush to hear it put so boldly. Its consequence is the acceptance of whatsoever is in the text which comports with our own "enlightened" view of matters. Or that in the text is taken to be meaningful which may be thus appropriated—all else belongs to an outmoded garb of colorful expression perhaps fitting for a benighted age but no longer needful for our adulthood. We should remember the way in which the nineteenth century quests for Jesus produced pictures of Jesus as the exemplar of nineteenth century virtues: Jesus as the exemplar of bourgeois morality, Jesus as the purveyor of reasonable and civilized ethical principles. We need not look back to the nineteenth century for such self-portraits in the guise of history, however. If Jesus the moralist has not yet disappeared from our theology (he certainly holds sway in main-line Protestant churches), we may also note Jesus the revolutionary and Jesus the existentialist competing for our attention.

Are we to conclude from this then that the biblical texts serve simply as a mirror in which we able only to see ourselves? Shall we understand them as a series of complex verbal Rorschach Blots whose exposition reveals much about the expositor and nothing about the object of exposition?[13] It would seem so, yet the consequence would be serious indeed. Having designated these texts as the source of our self-understanding and made them normative for interpretation, we should only have created the illusion of a norm which is indeed passive to every interpretation. We are then the authors of the texts' meaning, and to the extent to which that is true, we no longer have hope of discovering from these texts something which we do not already know. Such a position may indeed be made into an epistemological principle. We necessarily approach the text with questions derived from our prior understanding. This determines what it is possible for us to hear from the text. Now this is an insight of fundamental importance for illuminating the character of the act of understanding. It is derived from Heidegger, informs Bultmann's denial of the possibility of an objective presuppositionless exegesis, and serves as the basis of Gadamer's monumental treatment of hermeneutics. Put in this way, it makes clear that our interest in the text shapes our reading of it. Who we are and who we understand ourselves to be is constitutive of what the text may have to say to us.

Yet if this is left without qualification we find ourselves cut off from correction by the text. We are then, as I have suggested, the authors of its meaning[14] and no real process of interpretation has occurred at all. Do our presuppositions then entirely determine the meaning of the text (in which case we might profitably dispense with the text altogether), or does the text itself help to shape, correct, or widen the pre-understanding, thereby itself contributing the meaning of our interpretation? It is upon this latter road that we must travel in attempting to give an adequate account of interpretation.

To be sure, a move is made in this direction by pointing to the way in which what undergirds both text and interpretation is a kind of human experience of life (Dilthey), which provides the basis for the possibility of mutuality of meaning. Whatever its antiquity and peculiarity, the text is authored by another human being and brings that person's experience of life and world to expression. While the horizon of meaning in which that text stands and which it brings to expression may be more or less remote from our own, it still stems from the experience of a life and world which, as human, must be in some respects akin to our own. If we are utterly the prisoners of our pre-understanding, then not only is the interpretation of a text from antiquity impossible, but also the possibility of understanding a contemporary is rendered ultimately unintelligible. If our theory of interpretation commits us to supposing that the text cannot correct or alter our pre-understanding, but that pre-understanding authors the meaning of the text, then we are ultimately driven toward a kind of solipcism in which the world of texts and voices is but a complex echo chamber of our own thoughts and prejudices. But how then did we come to have thoughts and prejudices? Do they derive from the spontaneous generation of ideas in some primeval mental swamp or have they not been derived from hearing and reading and seeing with the aid of a language we have not created but learned?

An adequate theory of interpretation then must surely take account of the way in which meaning is constituted, in part, by our pre-understanding. But it must also make some room (however large or small) for the role of the text (or speaker) in contributing to that meaning. The only way to procure a space for the voice of the text in our interpretation is by careful attention to its structure, to the modalities of its meanings as exhibited in the way its language functions internally. The consequence of such careful attention may be that it will come to seem more rather than less alien to our own perceptions and prejudices. The classic example of such careful exegesis is that of Johannes Weiss who, though he was and remained a liberal theologian, permitted the text to say something quite alien to the presupposition of liberal theology (namely, to represent the kingdom of God not as an immanent moral principle but a catastrophic end to history).[15] Yet it is precisely the same sort of attentiveness which is required of us if we are to permit the otherness of the text (or of a friend) to stand over against us in such a way as to alter our own perspective— enlarge it and transform it. This last point bears some emphasis. The inability to read is the same as the inability to listen. Both (assuming no technical obstacle) stem from the persuasion that we have nothing more to learn, that we have no need or wish to hear any voice other than our own. Under such conditions we will have no option but either to dismiss other voices (regarding them as outmoded, unliberated, un-American, mythological, childish) or to coerce them upon the Procrustean bed of our own (intellectual) narcissistic desire.

We are frequently tempted to suppose that otherness must somehow be denied—that it is the enemy of understanding. Thus we shrink from the otherness of such a text. But otherness is the very foundation of understanding. We may be helped here if we attend to the way in which we deal with one another. It is no mark of friendship to reduce the other to a mere echo of ourselves. To the extent that friend or lover comes to be seen by us as simply an extension of ourselves, they cease to be human beings and become the projection and mirror of our fantasy. Candor would compel us to admit that we are perpetually tending toward this very reduction—that we are uneasy with any profound or even apparent difference between us and those we are close to in habits, opinion, or taste. Yet it is possible that we may also recognize from our experience occasions when the very otherness of the other prompted us to become more fully human through taking that difference into account—being prodded by it into a reconsideration of our own prejudices and practices, and led thereby into becoming, not the reflection of the other, but more truly ourselves in relation to that other.

In a similar way the otherness of the text, if we have taken the trouble to attend to it and recognize it, may be an occasion not of alienation but of new and unanticipated understanding of both the text and of ourselves. We short-circuit this process and short-change ourselves if we are impatient with the text—if we denounce its otherness or disguise it. For all of that, however, our interpretation of the text will bear the imprint of those pre-judgments, those prior understandings which we bring to it. We will not succeed in jumping out of our linguistic and conceptual skins into an altogether different perspective. Nor is this at all necessary or desirable, for the interpretation of a text does not mean the repetition of its meanings in the same form in which we found them.

Preoccupation with a fixed past is no more historical than preoccupation with our own present. Both reduce time to a point which is rendered immune to time. The past-time of the text and the present-time of interpretation are placed in reciprocal relation to one another. An interpretation which purports to escape from the present into a privileged past undermines the historical character of that past—makes it no longer a voice addressed to us but a remote conversation overheard by a tape-recorder. A response to a word addressed to us will bear the impress of our own context of hearing, just as it will also (if indeed it is a *response*) be pertinent to that which was said by the other. An adequate interpretation of the text will therefore bear the marks of the dialectic between the past (text) and the present (interpreter). To the extent that one or the other of these poles is muted or silenced no interpretation has taken place.

Interpretation then is a dialogue between past and present which

allows both parties to have their say. The process of such a
dialogue aims not only at the interpretation of the past on the part
of the present, but also the interpretation of the present on the
part of the past. The interpreter interprets the text, but only
insofar as the text is permitted to interpret the interpreter and the
interpreter's world. In order for these movements to occur, the
distance between past and present must be recognized rather than
abrogated by too hastily collapsing the past into the present (the
danger of existential interpretation) or collapsing the present into
the past (the danger of all varieties of orthodoxy). Perhaps the
most important contribution to the recognition of this salutary distance between past and present is made by the methods of historical
criticism. By these methods the text is placed resolutely into its
own context or horizon of meaning in such a way as to make clear
its distinctiveness of language and world view. If the matter is
allowed to drop here, however, no real dialogue has yet taken place,
and thus no theological interpretation. Only when we move from
disjunction to confrontation, mutual interrogation, and thus toward
mutual illumination, does interpretation actually take place. In
this way what Hans-Georg Gadamer calls a "fusion of horizons"[16]
occurs in which the horizon of meaning of the text and the horizon
of meaning of the interpreter overlap so as to produce a fresh
understanding of each, but in such a way as not to reduce the one
to the other. When this occurs then it is also appropriate to speak,
as Ebeling does, of a "word-event," in which that which came to
expression in the text comes to expression in the present, founding
afresh the world of meaning within which we have our lives in
the present and from the past.

It should be becoming clear that this does not occur by a one
way movement in which the text instructs us on the meaning of
the present, or the present instructs on the meaning of the text.
Both movements belong together in such a way as to prevent either
from becoming absolute. Any fully developed hermeneutics
(theory of interpretation) will need to give an adequate account of
each of these movements. Contemporary hermeneutics stresses the
role of pre-understanding (our situation within a present context
of meaning) in the interpretation, and thus may require some
correction in the direction of restoring to the text its own voice, its
own otherness, in the dialogic process constitutive of interpretation.

THE ROLE OF THE PAST

I have been indicating the relation which theology has to its own past and the way this relation impinges upon and helps to form its present. It must be emphasized that the meanings with which theology deals are meanings for the present. The concern of theology is not the preservation or conservation of the meanings of an ancient text or of the mythos it represents, but the elaboration of meaning for present existence. I have been emphasizing that the effective prosecution of this task entails a certain kind of relation to the past from which the mythos is received. But it is also necessary to cultivate as keen a perception as we are able of our contemporary world—for it is here that theology must perform its task.

Theological judgments must be made in the language and conceptuality available in contemporary culture. They must arise from and persuasively engage the texture of present experience, personal and social. They should reflect an awareness of and serious dialogue with insights derived from other kinds of inquiry into the meaning and character of human existence.

But why an inquiry into the past at all, why not concern ourselves solely with the present? I have already given some of the reasons for theology's peculiar preoccupation with a particular past. It may, however, help to supplement these with a consideration of the way in which our present is received from the past generally.

That we are constituted as persons by our own pasts is an insight which has grown to have increasing importance for psychotherapy. Much of our existence as persons and as a society, however, is deformed by the renunciation and repression of the past in favor of a present we can more easily control. We disown the past which forms us, as a testament to our pride in the extent of our prowess in managing and dominating the present. The cost involved in disowning our past is alienation from ourselves. The way of health, psychic and social, lies through the reclamation of our personal and corporate past, not in order to dwell in the past, but to inform and enrich the present.

Something like this recognition of the importance of past seems to be emerging as a focus of the humanities. We may note that the primary movements of humanistic studies and of artistic creation seem today to be poised between a radical recourse to the primal past and an uncertain submersion in a fleeting present. It is the former characteristic which is, I believe, most notable. If we look, for example, at the philosophy of Martin Heidegger, we will notice philosophy turning back upon itself in quest of its own origin in the primal interrogation of being. Heidegger struggles against and through a language sedimented with the accumulated debris of the intervening past to discover imbedded at its etymological foundation a primary deposit of ontological insight. So also in the case of the psychoanalytic movements founded by Freud and Jung. In the case of Freud, the procedure is an archeological excavation which seeks to discern in the accumulated debris of fantasy, dream, and inadvertant behavior, the traces of an original dynamic of repression posited in the image of a primal scene. Jung attempts to push the archeological excavation into even more primordial chambers of the unconscious to discover the archetypal patterns of a collective unconscious emerging from chthonic depths. We may also notice here how the discipline of anthropology (the study of humanity) is indissolubly connected with an archeological and primitivistic context and direction of inquiry.

Mircea Eliade,[17] whose own researches into the phenomenology of religion fall well within the range of this archeological quest, notes that much contemporary artistic creation may be understood as a turning of art back upon itself. Its primary elements of color and line (painting), mass and nascent shape (sculpture), kinetic rhythm (rock, acid and otherwise), and juxtaposition of sounds just hovering on the brink of noise (contemporary classical music), all testify to the fascination with the primary and primal disclosed through an archeological excavation of the founding elements of expression.

It is still more crucially important to understand the role which our own past plays in shaping the patterns of present experience. If we do not have a clear sense of the importance of a personal past, then the preoccupation of theology with its own past will always seem stultifying and even morbid. Through inquiring how it is that we experience significance in relation to our past we may gain helpful insight into the character and importance of theology's concern for the past.

As a people Americans are perhaps the least concerned with the past. Generations of expansion have taught us to think of the past as irrelevant to our concern for present and future. Ethnic minorities have been assimilated at the cost of a repudiation of the past and its exchange for the American dream of upward mobility. Any clinging to the past could only be a hindrance to this future-oriented economic mobility. In this as in a great many other ways Americans have been taught to disdain and disown the past—to live altogether in a present poised for its leap into the future.

Since the time of Freud, however, we have begun to learn that the past cannot simply be cast off as a snake sheds its skin. Rather the past—in this context especially the personal past—determines the patterns of our experience. The unremitting contingency of the events and context of birth and initial socialization stamp us forever with their contour. The denial or repression of these formative forces serves only to increase their subterranean power, and to ensnare us all the more in the dynamics of their manipulation. Only by learning painfully to own our past, to appropriate it, do we gain, not mastery over it, but that modicum of liberty within it that is our rightful portion.

The appropriation of the past makes possible alternative perceptions of the present; some modest leverage is gained upon the present and thereby the capacity to modify it in the direction of a more humane future. In this way the concern for an understanding of and responsibility for the past serves to enrich the meaning of present experience.

The concern which theology evidences for its own past is not therefore at odds with the character of our common quest for meaning in existence. Theology does not seek to repeat or remain within its own past. Indeed, some theology may seek to reverse or invert fundamental symbolic structures received from the past, as in the case of the theology of Thomas Altizer. But theology does need to confront its own past critically and responsibly if it is not to consign itself to the hegemony of the present or the insensate reiteration of its past.

The concern of theology for the authority of the past is not therefore a flight from the present, but constitutes its peculiar way of gaining a leverage upon that present so as to inform and shape the experience of contemporary faith. In this it parallels rather than contradicts the attempt to discover meaning in existence through an appropriation of our personal past. It is the recognition of this parallel which grounds the emergence of an autobiographical style of theological reflection in which the Christian story is interpreted by, and at the same time interprets, one's own story.[18]

In this way fundamental theological judgments are brought into dynamic relation to the events of one's own history. The theological terms are thus located in the drama of existence and existence is illumined by the received symbols. The consequence is an enrichment of both.

The relationship of theological reflection to autobiographical reflection is no novelty in the history of theology. From the *Confessions* of Augustine to the *Letters and Papers* of Bonhoeffer, the importance of anchoring theological reflection in the context of one's own history and experience has been amply attested. The increasing awareness of the importance of this approach for the teaching of theology may signal a rejuvenation of theological discourse. The dangers against which the previous chapter warned must be warned against in this context as well: the danger of reducing theological reflection to a mere echo of autobiographical data on the one hand, and that of imposing a rigid theological schema upon the data of one's memory and experience on the other. Nevertheless, the possibilities for a mutually enriching dialogue between autobiographical reflection and the appropriation of a communal past are authentically grounded in the recognition on each side of this dialectic that meaning is not the product of a here and now severed from history and memory, but is the contribution of a fruitful interaction between present and past.

NOTES

1. Van A. Harvey, *The Historian and the Believer*, p. 246.
2. Chapter five above.
3. For a discussion of the emergence of the canon see any standard Introduction to the New Testament.
4. For a discussion of various ways of understanding the character of Scripture cf. G. Gloege's article on the Bible in *Die Religion in Geschichte und Gegenwart* (3rd edition), I, pp. 1142-7.
5. I am indebted to Herman Ridderbos for this designation. Cf. his "The Canon of the New Testament" in Carl Henry ed. *Revelation and the Bible* (Grand Rapids: Baker, 1958), pp. 190-201.
6. For the presentation of a contemporary Catholic perspective cf. Yves M. J. Congar, *Tradition and Traditions* (New York: The Macmillan Company, 1967).
7. Gerhard Ebeling, *The Word of God and Tradition*, trans S. M. Hooke (Philadelphia: Fortress Press, 1968), pp. 11-31.
8. Karl Barth, *Protestant Theology in the Nineteenth Century* (Valley Forge; Judson Press, 1973), p. 17.
9. Gerhard Ebeling, *op. cit.*, p. 111.
10. Gerhard Ebeling's article in *Die Religion in Geschichte und*

Gegenwart (3rd edition) on "Hermeneutik" (Vol. III, pp. 242 ff) remains an invaluable source.

11. For a discussion of the positions of these pioneering figures cf. Richard E. Palmer, *Hermeneutics: Interpretation Theory in Schleiermacher, Dilthey, Heidegger and Gadamer* (Evanston: Northwestern University Press, 1969).

12. An excellent discussion of the priority of the oral over the literal may be found in Walter J. Ong, *The Presence of the Word* (New York: Clarion, 1970).

13. This position was first brought forcefully to my attention by Manfred Hoffman, my friend and teacher at Emory University.

14. Cf. E. D. Hirsch, Jr., *Validity in Interpretation* (New Haven: Yale University Press, 1967).

15. Johannes Weiss, *Jesus' Proclamation of the Kingdom of God,* trans. R. H. Hiers and D. L. Holland (Philadelphia: Fortress Press, 1971).

16. Hans Georg Gadamer, *Wahrheit und Methode* (Tübingen: J. C. B. Mohr, 1965).

17. Mircea Eliade, *Myth and Reality* (New York: Harper and Row, 1963), pp. 181 ff.

18. For explorations into the relationship of autobiography and theology cf. John Dunne, *The Search for God in Time and Memory* (New York: Macmillan, 1969); Michael Novak, *Ascent of the Mountain, Flight of the Dove* (New York: Harper and Row, 1971); and Harvey Cox, *The Seduction of the Spirit* (New York: Simon and Schuster, 1973).

Chapter 8

Individual and Communal

It must be admitted from the first that theological reflection as a responsibility of the church seems somewhat foreign and alien in the contemporary American setting. A distinguishing characteristic of American Protestant theology is its very separation from the ecclesiastical context. Catholic and Orthodox theologies almost invariably take seriously the character of the community out of which they speak, even if only to attack it. The Protestant theology of Europe usually exhibits a close tie to the actual situation in the church and this seems to be the case with respect also to third-world theology. Thus, in suggesting a positive and close relationship between theological reflection and a community of faith, I am aware of coming into conflict with one of the distinguishing characteristics of the American theological context. Yet I am persuaded that much of the poverty of American theology and church life is due to the way in which they have been isolated from one another. In this chapter no more than a beginning can be made in suggesting the importance of a relationship to a community of faith for theological reflection. Yet such a beginning may open the way for further exploration of this theme as a means of improving the adequacy of our theological judgments.

Students in college or seminary who commence upon the tasks of theological reflection frequently do so out of a sense of the inadequacy of the life of the church out of which they come. At its very beginning, therefore, theological reflection is fraught with frustration with and even antipathy toward the church. Thus it is not *in* the church but *against* the church that one attempts to work out the meaning of the symbols of faith. This situation is inevitable and indeed helpful in the process of shaking words and symbols loose from the contexts in which their meaning is often buried for us by habit, misuse, or unfortunate associations. It may therefore be a necessary and beneficial stage in theological reflection. But if this situation of antagonism is not transcended, then the theological insight won at such cost of personal struggle and labor is used not to nourish the community but to punish it. The community is thereby sentenced to further impoverishment of understanding while the theological reflection itself loses its essential grounding in the experience of a community and thus becomes abstract, arcane, and in the narrow and pejorative sense, "academic."

INDIVIDUALITY AND RELATIONALITY

One of the reasons that the assertion of the responsibility of theology to and for the church may seem at first repugnant to us is that we unconsciously assume a necessary alienation of the individual from the group. We have been taught to prize individuality above all things and to understand society, especially in its institutional forms, as, at best, a necessary evil. The title of Reinhold Niebuhr's study of Christian ethics, *Moral Man and Immoral Society*, seems to be but the statement of a commonsense view of the relative value of the individual as opposed to society. The assertion of the responsibility of theology to the church seems therefore to entail an abdication of one's personal responsibility, and the exchange of a greater value (that of individual integrity) for a lesser one (that of society's approval). It is not difficult to rehearse in our minds a multitude of examples which illustrate the way in which society is in the wrong as against the individual. The demands and pressures of society seem inevitably to stifle novelty, creativity, and insight. This is not less true of the church, considered as an institution, than of any other social organization.

All of this remains valid and indeed needs to be learned again and again in the world in which we live. Yet if it is not carefully and critically understood it may lead us to suppose that the individual is or ought to be autonomous and independent from the social nexus. The consequence of a high value being placed upon the individual as opposed to society is not only "democracy" but also the worse excesses of laissez-faire capitalism. When value is located in the individual alone the consequences are not necessarily liberating. The absolute individual may become the absolute despot.[1]

What is ultimately at stake here is our vision of the fundamental character of human existence and thus of human meaning. Is

human existence at its most basic level independent of the nexus
of relationships in which we find ourselves?   Are these relationships external and accidental to who we really are?   Or is it the
case that we are constituted by these relationships—that who we
are is a product of relationships to other persons and the broader
social nexus in which they stand?

The notion of our independence from other persons underlies
the ethos of rugged individualism which is the peculiar American
adaptation of Enlightenment sensibility.   But this individualism is
rendered in a far more sophisticated fashion by some of the varieties
of existentialism which concentrate upon the individual in inwardness.   Despite the great difference between rugged individualism
and existential inwardness, they may both contribute to an understanding of ourselves as fundamentally individual, and thus as
related to others only incidentally or externally.

In this context then the meaning of existence veers toward the
idiosyncratic, private, and incommunicable.   We tend to think of
ourselves as refugees from alien social structures.   We jealously
guard our individuality and interiority from the vulgar and con-
stricting encroachments of communal norms and standards.   The
community, especially an established or structured community, can
be seen as the enemy—ever threatening to swamp the tiny vessel
of our personhood in an angry sea of group and crowd pressures.

Yet if we attend to the character of meaning, if we are attentive
to the events in which meaning happens, we very quickly begin to
see that this picture falsifies our experience though it also represents
some features of it.   We may discover that meaning, even the most
intimate meaning, derives from a social nexus.

One of the ways in which this may begin to become clear to
us is through a consideration of the nature of language and its
relationship to the meanings by which we orient our existence.
There can be no question but what language may often be experienced as truncating and distorting those meanings.   Certainly we
all have occasion to note the way in which our meanings are be-
trayed by language, or seem to be coerced by it into forms which
have lost their power to convey.   We may become wary of language
and chary in its use.

Yet a withdrawal into silence does not preserve meaning intact.
An unexpressed and inexpressible meaning is no longer clearly a
meaning at all.   It is through our appropriation of the world of

language that the question of meaning arises at all for us. It is through language that our world of patterned (and thus significant) experience comes into view. Experiences which might otherwise be lost amid the confusion of sheer succession are highlighted for us by the words which, however inadequately, name them, sort them, identify them. It is language which allows us to attend to experiences of love, to distinguish these experiences from those of manipulation, and to communicate to ourselves and to others the rich texture of the experience. The refusal to articulate such experiences for ourselves or for others is a refusal to attend to them, to prize them, to live by them and from them.

We are thus poised in our experience between the insufficiency of language and the necessity of speech. This ambiguity in our linguisticality may indeed be taken to signify a central and ineradicable ambiguity in our existence. Certainly our linguisticality is the most pervasive manifestation of the symbolicity which causes Cassirer to identify our species as *homo symbolicum*—the symbol-using animal. We may recall the suggestion made early in this essay that existence be understood as receiving expression through images and symbols. This pressing-out of existence is in the direction of consciousness but also communication. Consciousness apart from the matrix of communication is impossible. Meaning happens when, through the symbol, reality (including the reality of our existence) is mediated to consciousness and thus communicated or made available for communication. Most of us have probably had the experience of only understanding some dim intuition of meaning in the process of trying to communicate it to a friend. In attempting to communicate we first become truly conscious of that meaning. That experience may serve to indicate how closely meaning is tied to language.

But if it is true that meaning—including the most passionately subjective meaning—is tied to our use of language, then we are brought to the point of seeing how thoroughly social is the occurrence of meaning. We are, in our earliest education, inserted into an already existing world of language. We do not create that world, that system of language. We might instead say that it creates us. The words and syntax which ever after will mold and pattern our perception are—so far as we are concerned—simply given. Whatever theories we may develop about the origin or development of language it is clear that it is there prior to our own experience and volition. And it is there precisely as a social and public reality. Through immersion in the world of language we are drawn inexorably into a social world. Thereby we acquire a distinctively human consciousness and the ability to interrogate ourselves and our world for meaning. But this we do through the fundamentally socializing process of acquiring a language.

If linguisticality is taken as a decisive clue to the character of our existence, it becomes clear that society is not only chronologically but also *logic*ally prior to the individual. The meanings by which we live are fundamentally social meanings discovered, received, expressed through the language which is received from the community within which we live. For the most part the meanings by which we live are meanings sedimented in a linguistic tradition which is mediated to us socially Even when new meaning emerges through a creative innovation in that linguistic tradition, the force of that innovation depends upon its contrast to that tradition. So, for example, in the case of metaphor or parable which alters our commonplace perception. The alteration of perception is mediated by a breech in the conventions of language which remains dependent upon those conventions (in order to evoke the contrast) and thus is dependent upon the socially received meanings while offering a new and perhaps contrary meaning. So it is any rate with the poetic use of language.[2]

The emergent study of the sociology of knowledge casts further light upon the essentially social character of human meaning. We frequently operate with the notion that knowledge is arrived at through the independent inquiry of the individual. But, as Berger and Luckmann have shown, knowledge is itself a social product.[3] The presuppositions about reality which shape and mold all inquiry are social in character. This means that reality is itself constructed upon the framework of social conventions. From the everyday reality of commonsense to the specialized reality of the scientist, that in terms of which the real is distinguished from the unreal has a thoroughly social and thus conventional character.

When, in an earlier chapter, I described what was called the objective-manipulative consciousness, I was then describing a set of conventions widely shared in modern Western society. These conventions determine the way in which reality is viewed by members of that society (or those societies). But the conventions have their grounding or foundation not in reality itself, but rather in the society and the individuals who constitute that society and act out of those conventions. These conventions themselves are inculcated institutionally in educational systems which are legitimized by the conventions. (So, in a university one must show how the study of religion may be an objective discipline—it helps if one uses computers—and, to the extent one is successful in this enterprise, the department of religion is legitimated and itself becomes an inculcator of this particular social construction of reality.)

What this suggests is that any act of knowing will have as its basis a communal construction of reality which determines the legitimacy of what is known. These constructions determine in advance the reality or unreality of a particular mode and object of inquiry. This is not to invoke some ultimate skepticism about reality and knowing, but to point to the social character of all our knowledge and to the way in which reality itself is patterned for us by a social construction of that reality. This suggests then the very real importance of community in any process of understanding and makes clear that even here the individual does not and cannot stand alone.

If this seems rather abstract it is possible to place it in a different context—that of dialogue. It is in dialogue with the other that we discover, communicate, and celebrate the meanings of our existence. Such meanings are not idiosyncratic and private. They happen between persons. This is the fundamental insight of thinkers such as Feuerbach, Martin Buber, and Ferdinand Ebner[4] who have done so much to bring the relational character of human existence (and thus of human meaning) to our attention under the rubric of the I-thou. The fundamental meanings of our life are woven of the encounter with the other and this encounter occurs, as these thinkers all emphasize, through dialogue. The meaning of our life is spun out of the concrete words of address and response: judgment, approval, promise, covenant, wish, forgiveness, love. In the events in which these and other words are addressed to or by us our life takes a new turn, a fresh meaning.

These few indications could be indefinitely expanded if our intent were to elaborate a dialogical model of meaning. Rather than that, however, I want only to point to the way in which at its most concrete level the meaning of our existence is anchored in encounters with other persons, as a way of suggesting that any enterprise which has as its aim the uncovering of meaning for life cannot subscribe to a view which severs the individual from the social contexts of relationality.

The question of the character of theological reflection may seem to have receded behind the questions of linguisticality, sociology of knowledge, and relationality. These are, however, three ways of pointing to the necessity that theological reflection as a search for meaning must be understood as taking place, not in the isolate autonomy of individual reflection, but in a context heavily determined by social and relational factors.

It should, moreover, be clear that this in no way entails an absorption of the person into the social nexus. It is precisely characteristic of the personal nature of human being and meaning that it is forged within and by the help of the structures of language, social perception, and relational communication. The theoretical and practical disjunction of individual and society is a fundamental distortion of the character of human being.

If we now rejoin earlier discussions of the character of imagination this becomes all the more clear. In the third chapter I noted that imagination is never simply confined within the precincts of the individual, the private, the idiosyncratic. Instead it is at its very center a profoundly social and even collective activity and power. In the most private and apparently idiosyncratic images of the dream, Jung discerns the paradigms of collective experience residing in the "collective unconscious." But these are not simply impersonal patterns—they are the conveyors of meaning which aim at the healing transformation of human consciousness and behavior. They are a potent fusion of the personal and the most comprehensively collective. Similarly the example of artistic creation was cited to indicate the way in which the passionately personal and the universally meaningful are wed in the poem or painting. The impersonal is uninteresting and banal, but the personal communicates vividly and directly to a community of readers, viewers, or hearers. Even in the case of science, which we so readily understand in terms of autonomous reason, there is an adherence to and labor within the parameters of a shared paradigm which constitutes the community of scientists.

But it is in the case of the religious imagination that I have already had occasion to stress the particular emphasis upon the communal. As I noted earlier, it was Durkheim who first established the thesis that religion is fundamentally a social, communal phenomenon. While his thesis has had to be modified in detail it is clear that it is impossible to separate religion from community in such a way as to speak in any but a derivative sense of an individual's religion. The function of a mythos is to establish a community within which the communication of ultimate meanings takes place. This means that the reality designated by a mythos is dependent upon the existence of a community apart from which it does not function as a reality. A religious mythos is a way of patterning the perception of the world for a community, and it is only in that way that it functions to pattern perception for those who are a part of that community.

CHURCH AND THEOLOGIAN

We may now turn to a more direct consideration of theological reflection. What has gone before serves to ground the thesis that *theological reflection is necessarily reflection on behalf of and within a community of faith.* That thesis rendered as bluntly as possible is: *theology exists for the sake of the church.* Despite the fact that this thesis may seem at once to be dependent upon Barth it is, in fact, the governing principle of theological reflection generally. This may be illustrated by two theses taken from Schleiermacher's introduction to the *Brief Outline on the Study of Theology.*[5]

> § 5 Christian theology, accordingly, is that assemblage of scientific knowledge and practical instruction without the possession of which a united leadership of the Christian Church, i.e., a government of the church in the fullest sense, is not possible.
> § 6 When this same is acquired and possessed without relation to the "government" of the Church, it ceases to be theological and devolves to those sciences to which it belongs according to its varied content.

I cite these theses because we are not accustomed to associate Schleiermacher with the position which they articulate and because a more straight-forward expression of that position is scarcely to be found elsewhere. That the position is given expression by Schleiermacher, the founder of modern theology, and that the position is not there incidentally but as the foundation of theological reflection, indicates the general and essential nature of this position —namely, that theology exists for the sake of the church.

That theology as a reflection upon the meaning of human existence should situate itself in relation to a community, rather than
simply in relation to the individual, should by now seem inevitable,
given our prior discussion of the social character of human existence
and human meaning. That it undertakes this reflection by way of
recourse to the products of the religious imagination is all the more
indicative of its location within a community constituted by that
mythos. Insofar as reflection upon the mythos abstracts itself from
the community of faith constituted by that mythos, it ceases to be
theological reflection at all. This does not mean that such reflection
is illegitimate or impossible or unnecessary: only that it is not yet
theological reflection. Theological reflection as a reflection upon
the mythos is a reflection founded in that mythos, and thus located
within the community which is formed, sustained, and corrected
by the mythos.

But if we were to leave the matter here then enormous problems
and possible misunderstandings would arise. What then becomes
of the responsibility of the theologian? Is the theologian only the
"mouthpiece" of the church? The assertion that theology exists
for the sake of the church then only serves to place us in a position
to raise questions about that relationship and responsibility. It is
not itself an answer to such questions. Some of these questions,
then, need to be clarified, if not answered, if we are to begin to
grasp what is at stake in the assertion of the relationship of theology
to the church.

I began this chapter by pointing to the way in which theological
reflection frequently has its inception in frustration or discontent
with the church. Does this mean then that the reflection which is
thereby engendered is not or cannot be theological reflection? If
we look carefully at the situation, we can see readily that there is
no necessary contradiction between saying that theological reflection
is over against, as well as on behalf of, the church. The symbols
and stories upon which one reflects in this case are symbols and
stories which have been transmitted to the would-be theologian by
and within a church. Thus even when theological reflection is
undertaken in order to gain distance upon the conventional meanings of Christian symbols and texts, one is already indebted to the
community which preserves and transmits the mythos.

But how is it that this reflection, which so often emerges over
against the church, exists nevertheless for the sake of the church? It

should first be noted that we are not dealing here with an extra-ordinary situation. The meaning of the Christian mythos neces-sarily stands over against the community which it sustains. In an earlier chapter I pointed to the way in which critical reflection is necessitated by the Christian mythos itself. Theological reflection as this critical reflection is but one of the successors to the long line of attempts to "test the spirits," to abolish graven images, to expose the idols, and to apply what Tillich has called the Protestant principle. To say that theology exists for the sake of the church then in no way means that the theologian is obliged to be the docile articulator of prevailing opinion within the community of faith. The attempt to wrest the meanings of the mythos free of the confining structures and conventional languages in which they are domesticated is a continuing and necessary characteristic of theological reflection. It is just this activity which may be desig-nated as "for the sake of the church." The ossification or banaliza-tion of the meanings of the Christian mythos must ultimately mean the disintegration of the community which is sustained by them. To the extent that theological reflection stands over against the process of banalization and ossification—to that extent it is func-tioning on behalf of and for the sake of the community sustained by these images.

Now this should indicate that speaking of theology as standing within and existing for the sake of the church in no way diminishes the personal responsibility of the theologian. A theology in which one simply claims to be reporting what a number of Christians think about a certain matter is a branch of sociology or history, but it is not yet theological reflection in the strict sense. By this I mean that theological reflection arises in response to the symbols or images of the mythos, and that that response cannot be an altogether impersonal one. To speak responsibly or to assume responsibility here means to respond to a word which has been addressed to oneself. If I have been right in suggesting that theo-logical reflection is a reflection upon the meaning of our existence, then it is not appropriate to disclaim personal responsibility for one's articulation or interpretation of that meaning. Thus it is necessary that one step in theological reflection be an interrogation of the meaning of the symbol for me. To the extent that that ques-tion is evaded I have not responded to the mythos as mythos and thus have not prosecuted the task of genuine theological reflection.

This is indeed one of the peculiarities of theological reflection within a world in which we are usually told to bracket or postpone the question: what does this really matter to me? I suspect that is one reason that so many students find theology to be such a potentially worthwhile and even exhilarating enterprise. It is one enterprise in which one must and may perpetually wrestle with the question of personal meaning.

But it is crucial to theological reflection that personal meaning be related to communal meaning. The theologian is not the author of the mythos upon which she or he reflects. The mythos is received from the past and from a community. Nor is that all, for the function of the mythos, as has been noted, is to serve as the basis for the communication or sharing of meaning and this functions to create and sustain community. The mythos functions in this way only insofar as the interpretation of its meaning does in fact foster this communication and thus engender afresh the community sustained by the mythos. Theological reflection grounded in the mythos then will have as its aim, directly or indirectly, the reformation and renewal of the community which is sustained by the mythos.

If this is so then it will mean that the study of theology cannot be isolated from the life of the church without serious damage to both theology and the church. This clearly does not mean that theology must somehow or other compromise itself in order to have a less troubled relation to the church. That would certainly not be a strategy which could be pursued for the sake of the church. It would simply be a public relations activity pursued for the sake of theology (to keep it from coming under attack by the church). Theology cannot cease to be critical and still remain theology. It does mean, however, that the critical reflection which is crucial for theology must be carried on in dialogue with the communities which are or purport to be sustained by that same mythos which also gives rise to theological reflection. This means that in the course of theological reflection one must in some way or other take that community into account. Of course, if that were to happen in any widespread way it might mean a significant alteration in the way in which theological reflection is actually carried out—at least in mainline Protestant America. For the church too it would have important consequences, especially in summoning the church to an identity less dissipated in program and instituttional self-preservation and perpetuation and more grounded in and focused upon the distinctive mythos which is its only appropriate ground for existing in the world.

How one takes into account the community of faith is something which is inappropriate to specify at this point since it must itself depend upon the way in which one understands the Christian community. This is the theme of ecclesiology and therefore a full discussion of it would be theological rather than pre-theological. Nevertheless, in the doing of theology one may and must inquire of oneself: on whose behalf and for the sake of whom am I reflecting? In what sense is my reflection related both positively and negatively to the communities of faith? Where is the community within which and for which I undertake the disciplines of reflection?

The raising of this question already confronts us with the difficulty of specifying the character, parameters, or location of that community or those communities which may be vaguely indicated by the term church. Are we to take this term as a referring to that third of the world's population which is at least nominally Christian? Are we to take it as referring to one congregation or group of congregations with which we are acquainted? Do we refer here to the manifest churches or to the world as latent church (Tillich)? Do we mean the institutionally visible church or the invisible church of true believers? Or is it perhaps that small group of close associates with whom we are able to share, and which itself provokes our most urgent tasks of reflection? The point here is not to insist upon any one of these as the one best suited to answer to the necessity that our reflection be carried on in relation to a community of faith. Instead I want only to insist that insofar as our reflection is theological in nature it needs to be grounded within and directed toward a community of shared symbols. A theological education which encourages us to believe that theological reflection is something to be carried out in isolation, or that the results of that reflection might appropriately be a paper read only by ourselves and our teacher, vitiates that tie to a community which is constitutive of theological reflection.

What is crucial then is to keep steadily in view that theological reflection cannot adequately proceed in isolation from a context of shared meaning. So long as it is governed by a complete preoccupation with one's own questions, presuppositions, and perspective, it has not yet become a reflection genuinely responsive to the mythos upon which one purports to reflect, for that mythos functions not simply or perhaps even primarily as a response to one's own quest for meaning, but as the source and sustainer of community.

Despite the importance of locating our reflection within the polarity of community and individual, it is important not to suppose that these contrasting perspectives may be easily harmonized. The tension between them is not reducible to a simple solution. The disparity between them is most acutely pointed out by Soren Kierkegaard. Much of Kierkegaard's position depends upon working out the consequences of an opposition between the individual and the corporate, cultural, and institutional forms within which the individual may become lost. This opposition is virtually complete in the case of Christian existence.

Despite the cogency of Kierkegaard's attack upon the sheerly corporate character of Christendom,[6] it remains necessary to give an account of how the radical inwardness of faith can be related to the context of community. Kierkegaard himself, despite his notion of indirect communication, was aware of the necessity for proclamation. What is to be proclaimed in the community, however, is not one's own inwardness, but precisely the kerygmatic meanings which themselves place the individual before the radical demand for a choice in which existence is at stake. The reduction of this inwardness to corporate identity evades the *ad hominem* character of the Christian mythos. But the reduction of the corporate to inwardness eliminates the possibility of the mythos itself which alone confronts the person with a decision. Thus these two, the individual and the community, belong necessarily together and yet are in continuing and indissoluble tension with one another.

The task of theological reflection is to move between the contrasting perspectives of the individual and the community. That this movement is possible is suggested by the social character of personal being. That it is necessary is suggested by the way in which the Christian mythos functions as an address to the individual, summoning that person to the recognition and orientation of existence in and through the mythos, while at the same time founding and sustaining a community of faith constituted by the shared meanings of the mythos. If it is true in general that we exist only in relation to the other, it is particularly true that we exist on the basis of the Christian mythos only through being in relationship (love) with other persons.

This is not to say that the two perspectives, designated here as individual and communal, are reducible to a single perspective any more than past and present, or kerygmatic and phenomenological perspectives are reducible to one another or to some mysterious third term. Instead it means that theological reflection must move between these perspectives in such a way as to show that they do belong together without harmonizing them prematurely.

If in our culture, and especially in the academic setting within which theology continues to be studied, we are most tempted to reduce faith to the perspective of the individual, then we must all the more urgently insist upon the necessity of making the communal perspective a fundamental ingredient of our reflection. It is for this reason that it has seemed important to me to stress that theology takes place within and on behalf of the church.

But if we insist upon the way in which theological reflection must be situated within the community or communities sustained by the mythos, does that not mean that theology then becomes a variety of particularism speaking only its own ghetto language and thus is prevented from ever raising the question of human meaning in a radical or universal way? The question of the relationship of the particular and the universal is thus made all the more acute by our insistence that theology exists for the sake of the church. It is therefore to a discussion of that issue and of the place of theology in relation to the polarity of particular and universal that I will turn next.

NOTES

1. A connection forcefully brought forward by Karl Barth's analysis of the eighteenth century in *Protestant Theology in the Nineteenth Century*, pp. 39 ff.

2. Cf. Owen Barfield's *Poetic Diction*, 3rd ed., (Middletown: Wesleyan University Press, 1973).

3. Peter L. Berger and Thomas Luckmann, *The Social Construction of Reality* (Garden City: Anchor, 1967).

4. Ludwig Feuerbach, *Principles of the Philosophy of the Future*, trans. Manfred H. Vogel (New York: Bobbs-Merrill, 1966). Martin Buber, *I and Thou*, trans. Ronald Gregor Smith (New York: Scribner's, 1958). Perhaps the most influential of these thinkers for theology is Ferdinand Ebner, whose work is not yet translated into English.

5. Friedrich Schleiermacher, *Brief Outline on the Study of Theology*, trans. Terrence N. Tice (Richmond: John Knox Press, 1966), p. 20.

6. Soren Kierkegaard, *Attack upon Christendom*, trans. Walter Lowrie (Princeton: Princeton University Press, 1944).

Chapter 9

Particular and Universal

Since many of the issues which we have been considering in this essay bear upon the polarity which I refer to by the terms particular and universal, it may be useful to summarize them as they relate to this topic. Part Two began with a discussion of the relationship between critical reflection and conviction. That we have become accustomed to associate reflection with a universal standpoint is evidenced by the tendency to define the specific character of human being with the honorific titles of "homo sapiens" or "animal rationale." These titles indicate that reason is that which is most generally and universally human. Clearly, conviction particularizes, divides, and separates humanity into different and often warring camps. Thus, in the previous discussion the polarity of conviction and reflection corresponds roughly to the present polarity of particular and universality. It is the dogmatic movement of thought which corresponds to conviction which often brings upon itself the charge of particularism over against the phenomenological reflection which aims at the universal structure of human experience. Yet as we saw, these two directions of thought, dogmatic and phenomenological, seem to require one another.

In the discussion of past and present the stress upon the reference of theological reflection to a particular past represented by the Christ event and mirrored in the priority of Scripture over tradition similarly anticipates our present concern. But it is not as though reference to the past stands for the particular, while reference to the present stands for the universal. As was indicated in that discussion, reference to the past (indeed to a particular past) can help to deliver reflection from the provincialism and thus the particularism of the present. Nevertheless, the point of reference to a particular past (the past represented by the Christian mythos) itself raises the issue of particularity, for it is in the

148

name of the definiteness and discreteness of meaning that it was invoked. But does this not mean that we are tying our use of language to a constrictive and restrictive tradition which will prevent us from emcompassing the breadth of contemporary experience?

The discussion of individual and communal closed upon a similar note. If theological reflection is to be situated within the Christian community, does this not condemn us to speaking a ghetto language? Certainly our ordinary way of thinking about society is to think of it as placing limitations upon an otherwise unfettered and universal individuality. Thus, universality and individuality are linked together as the twin stars of our enlightenment produced ethos.

In each of these discussions, then, the question of the relationship of particularity (conviction, past, communal) to universality (reflection, present, individual) has already been broached. In each of those discussions, I have maintained that theological reflection must hold these contrasting perspectives together if it is not to result in the abandonment of its tasks of reflecting upon the Christian mythos and human existence. In this chapter I will attempt to show that particularity and universality belong together, and that it is only by holding them together (without, however, resolving the tension between them) that we are able to pursue the tasks of theological reflection. It will be necessary, in the first place, to indicate the way in which this question is a question about human meaning generally. I will then suggest the way in which this polarity is grounded in the nature of a mythos and in the structure of the Christian mythos. Some reflections upon what it means to exist and reflect within this tension will conclude the chapter.

UNIVERSALITY AND PARTICULARITY IN LIFE

The tension between particularity and universality is by no means peculiar to theological reflection. It may be illustrated in the history of literature and art, in the development of philosophical reflection on the nature of being, in the tensions of social and political life. The trap into which it is easy to fall is to suppose, however, that it is only in the case of religious life and theological reflection that we are required to think and act within certain prescribed parameters. Thus, since the Enlightenment, particularism and religion have tended to be linked together and unfavorably contrasted with the universal and all-encompassing horizons of reason, science, and general toleration. This attitude, which has its origins in the reaction against the decimating conflicts during the period of the religious wars, obscures for us, however, the ways in which particularity is as important for meaning as is universality. Rather than attempt to establish that thesis, however, I will illustrate it with reference to two situations in which particularity may claim importance alongside of universality.

The liberal dilemma. The first illustration is taken from the American ethos and may be termed the dilemma of the liberal mentality. The liberal mentality may be characterized as maintaining with respect to any person that the most important things about that person are those which are universally human characteristics. This emphasis upon what is common has itself been modified in American experience, which has had to accomodate itself to a population with widely divergent background. Thus, the attempt to develop a common language, culture, and vision (dream) for what is fundamentally an immigrant culture, has resulted in diverting attention away from the heritages, histories, traditions, and languages which divide us, toward whatever might serve as tokens of commonality. Much of the emphasis upon conformity which has dominated American life in the middle decades of this century may be traced to this emphasis. The assumption shared by the American experience and the liberal mentality is that particularity divides; commonality (and hence universality) unites.

The dilemma to which I earlier referred now emerges. The last decade of our experience has witnessed the emergent demand for a cultural and political recognition of the legitimate place of particularity. The rise to prominence of such slogans as "black power" and "black pride" has signaled the emergence into the public arena of women's groups, men's groups, gay power, and what Michael Novak has called the "rise of the unmeltable ethnics."[1]

What may be seen as common in these various movements is the assertion that one's humanity has not been taken into account at all if one is supposed to be simply a human being in general. Our humanity, that is to say, is as much a product of particularity (in this case cultural or sub-cultural, economic and political particularity) as it is composed of those elements which are or are asserted to be universally human. It is especially noteworthy that this emphasis has had to be made in the face of and thus over against our avowedly liberal stance. Thus, for example, the cry for black consciousness stands directly opposed not so much to overt racism as to the insistence of the liberal (white or black) that blackness is not important.

What I am attempting to point to here is not a solution of our cultural dilemmas but to indicate that a part of that dilemma is the necessity of finding a way to emphasize particular*ity* without that resulting in the divisiveness and antagonism associated with particular*ism*. Conversely, how are we able to emphasize what we take to be universally human without that resulting in the kind of tacit cultural imperialism which insists that everyone must be like us? Part of the crucial contribution of movements like black power is to expose the way in which the stressing of the universally human not only robs us of our particularity (and thus our humanity) but also conceals a covert cultural imperialism.

The existential choice. The importance of particularity may be illustrated at yet another level—the level of moral existence. Søren Kierkegaard protested vigorously against the tendency to subsume the individual under the crowd, the concrete under the abstract, the actual under the possible, the particular under the universal. Whether in the emerging mass societies of the mid-nineteenth century, or in the systematic philosophy of Hegel, he sought to turn the gaze of his reader to the actual and concrete and away from the hypnotizing effect of abstraction. The persistence and passion with which Kierkegaard pursued this task was grounded in his conviction that the loss of particularity entails the loss of truly human existence.

In his long early work *Either/Or*, Kierkegaard locates his problematic at the level of concrete choice.[2] By means of a series of letters and papers which present the self-portrait of a young aesthete and self-styled seducer, he illustrates existence which has lost its passion for the particular. In a second series of letters written to this young man by "Judge Wilhelm," the choice of particularity and thus of existence is depicted in rich detail.

The young aesthete lives in a world of multiple possibility and momentary attachment. Love, for him, is seduction—the manipulation of the other's desire and mood. Life is the moment, fleeting yet inexhaustible in variety. Judge Wilhelm is a married man.

For him life is choice, and love is steadfastness in that choice. Possibility may be multiple and inexhaustible, but the actual is singular, particular, and finite. Kierkegaard is here not playing an idle philosopher's game—he is wrestling with the way in which existence has meaning and is doing so autobiographically. The question of marriage was a real one for him, and in it is represented and concentrated the question of lifestyle and meaning.

Kierkegaard himself agrees with the fundamental point of Judge Wilhelm that existence is choice, that choice is an either-or, that decision means turning from the merely possible toward the particular. Such a turning means a renunciation of infinite variety which is always also empty of actuality because devoid of particularity.

We can see what is at stake here if we inquire of our own existence whether it is the infinite possibility of fantasy or the singularity of choice and deed which gives it meaning. This question directs itself toward many levels of our life. The choice of a vocation means the renunciation of a variety of possibilities in favor of a single actuality. Unless that choice is made, energy is dissipated in a number of directions with little significant effect. Similarly, in relationships we often have to choose between an array of possible relationships and the actualization of a few. That choice determines the level of relatedness which we will experience, ranging from momentary attachment to lifelong fidelity.

What I have been stressing is that existence as a human being entails the choices constitutive of particularity. This is not to deny the importance of multiple possibility and fleeting attachment, but simply to emphasize that existence constituted solely by unrealized possibility or dominated by idealized fantasy, is ultimately frivolous and empty. On this level then we may readily recognize the importance of particularity even when here too it means relinquishing the option of living in sheer possibility, however multiple or ideal. The question of particularity versus universality of standpoint in theological reflection has its counterpart in our life in the choice between the ideal possible world of fantasy and the particular and actual world of existence.

THE SACRED AND THE CONCRETE

I have been suggesting that the question of the relationship of particularity and universality is one of importance for a consideration of the meaning of human existence generally. I want now to turn to a consideration of the way in which this polarity is grounded in the nature of a mythos generally, and then to a consideration of the way in which the structure of the Christian mythos necessitates the situating of theological reflection within this polarity.

The character of a mythos. A mythos represents the presence of the sacred in the human world. As such it represents the juxtaposition of the particular and the universal. The work of Mircea Eliade and others in the phenomenology of religions is in large part a phenomenology of the particularization and localization of the sacred. Thus the identification of sacred space, sacred story, sacred rite, all locate the sacred at some special point of the life of the community. That the sacred is manifest or present at some point rather than others is the foundation of particularity in religion. Yet it is the sacred which is thus manifest. That is, it is the fundamental power or reality which founds the human world of meaning which manifests itself as this particular point. Thus the universal is present in the particular. Herein lies the possibility of discriminating between the religion of a group and other forms of its life. Malinowski has pointed out that even the most primitive societies have the distinction between, for example, religion and science.[3] The possibility of such a distinction is founded in the particularization of the sacred. Yet as I have maintained, the function of religion (and thus of a mythos) is to orient existence in relationship to all the horizons of meaning. Precisely because it is the presence of the sacred which is represented in the mythos, the various regions of experience and existence are knit together in a web of meaning within which the individual and group have their place. Thus, while a mythos locates the sacred at some point in space, story, rite, or object, it does so precisely in such a way as to bind together all of life in a unity.

But, one might ask, why is this necessary? Why is it the case that religion unites ultimate and universal meaning with particularity? The answer has to do with the nature of meaning itself. A meaning without contour and pattern is no meaning at all. In order to be able to say what something is we must also be able to say what it is not. If we are unable to do so, then meaning becomes vague and finally falls away into vacuity. When we turn our attention to ultimate meaning, that is, those meanings which determine the significance of our life, it becomes especially urgent that these be given some precise focus and pattern lest such meanings simply cease to exist, thereby plunging existence into darkness. The interest in discreteness of meaning is served by the particularization and localization of the sacred in the human world. But the presence of the sacred at some point in that world places existence within that world under the protective sign of its meaning. Thus the dialectic of particular and universal stands at the very heart of religion as represented by the mythos. If the particular is dissolved into the universal, meaning becomes vague and finally empty. But if the ultimate is simply particular then the regions of existence are not knit together (then the mythos could not orient existence) and the sacred is reduced to one region of existence, thereby eliminating its (sacred) character of founding the human world.

The character of the Christian mythos. If we turn to the Christian mythos we see how this dialectic is even more sharply focused. The structure of the Christian mythos is such as to focus the universal in the particular in an especially paradoxical way. On one level this is present in the eschatalogical preaching of Jesus and of the later church. Jesus announced the irruption of the kingdom of God through his own words and deeds. The image of the kingdom of God as the coming transfiguration of history itself represents a thoroughly universal horizon. It indicates the transformation of all that is through the coming of the one who created and will create anew all that is. Yet this universal scope is particularized, certainly in the proclamation of the early church (and probably, in an implicit way, by Jesus himself) in that it is tied to the ministry of Jesus. Thus Jesus is proclaimed in early Christian communities as the one in and through whom the salvation of God comes.

Subsequently, the development of Christology, culminating in the formulations of Nicea and Chalcedon, is the development of a conceptuality within which it is possible to bring to expression both the universality and ultimacy of Jesus' significance (fully God) together with the particularity and specificity of Jesus' message and destiny (the humanity of Jesus). The dialectic of particularity and universality is thus given expression as fundamental paradox. It is crucial to note that at virtually every stage of this development we can detect the way in which the titles which signify the universal and ultimate religious meaning in the Christian mythos are placed in relationship to Jesus. Thus it remains important that it is Jesus whose resurrection is announced, whose crucifixion is preached, whose coming is anticipated. This designation of Jesus as the locus of particularity has importance for the emergence of the mythos, for it is always by means of this reference that the attempt is made to prevent the mythos from being dissolved in the cauldron of Hellenistic (and later Teutonic) syncretism.

Yet it is not only particularity which is safeguarded in this way, for clearly it is crucial not to abridge the universality and ultimacy of meaning in order to guarantee the particularity of reference. Thus there is continuing attempt to say that what happens in Jesus is of import, not simply for a community, but for the world; that what comes to expression in the Christ-event is the fundamental structure of reality.

It has been suggested that the formulations of Chalcedon are negative—that is, these formulations indicate boundaries which may be crossed only at the cost of dissolving the specificity of the Christian mythos. In the terms which I am employing here it would be appropriate to say that what these formulations attempt to do is to prevent the abridgment or compromise of either particularity or universality. Thus they maintain that meaning is to be discovered only in the actual, the concrete, and the particular (remember the discussion of the structure of the Christian mythos in chapter five), but that the meaning thus located is not provincial or regional. Instead it is fundamental, ultimate, and universal. That is, no doubt, an audacious claim, but it is the task of theological reflection not to compromise such a claim but to elaborate its meaning for contemporary human existence.

IDENTITY AND RELEVANCE

What has gone before should serve to ground the thesis that theological reflection must proceed in such a way as to reflect the resolute particularity of the Christian mythos. The necessity for such particularity must be maintained, even at the risk of appearing particularistic in perspective. I have been attempting to suggest that this demand for particularity is grounded both in the nature of a quest for human meaning and in the structure of the Christian mythos. What now remains is to suggest some of the consequences of this thesis for theological reflection.

Contemporary theology has been described by Jürgen Moltmann

as situated in a dilemma which he calls the identity/relevance dilemma.[4] A theology which no longer has a sense of its peculiar identity tends to become, as I have suggested, amateur sociology, psychology, or history. Without a sense of identity it is lost among a myriad of possibilities to each of which it seems necessary to be relevant. But a theology which stresses its identity as a reflection upon the Christian mythos within the Christian community stands in the danger of becoming merely a ghetto language cut off from the existence and world which the Christian mythos purports to interpret and for which the Christian community exists.

If the second danger (identity without relevance) has been exemplified in the history of orthodox and conservative varieties of theology, the first (relevance without identity) certainly is exemplified in the situation of liberal theology and the liberal church.[5] The consequence of the inability to articulate the specifically Christian identity of liberal churches has resulted in a crisis of major proportions in main-line Protestantism. Much of this is due, I believe, to the failure to see that, for the Christian mythos at least, particularity is the correlate rather than the negation of universality.

Theological reflection must therefore be prepared to assert and warrant its particularity if it is to be of any real use to the church in its present dilemma, yet it must do so in such a way as not to abridge or truncate the universality of scope (and therefore relevance) of the meanings which it elaborates and interprets. Pretensions to universality apart from particularity result in a vagueness which vitiates meaning. Universality thus requires particularity. But the particularity of theological reflection also requires universality of scope since the meanings of the Christian mythos are not adequately reflected unless it is clear in what way they engage the totality of human experience in the world.

If particularity and universality require one another, it is also the case that their tension is irreducible. What that means is that theological reflection must move between two contrasting poles designated as identity and relevance, or particularity and universality, without simply compromising the interest and intent of either. This makes theological reflection dialectical in that it is a movement which produces no final synthesis (that would be apocalyptic lucidity) of the contrasting perspectives between which it moves.

If this is true then it indicates all the more the provisional character of theological judgments—a provisionality which, however, cannot be simply at odds with the demand for valid theological judgments. It is to a consideration of this theme that I will turn in the next chapter.

NOTES

1. Michael Novak, *The Rise of the Unmeltable Ethnics* (New York: Macmillan, 1972).
2. Søren Kierkegaard, *Either/Or*, trans. David F. Swenson (Garden City: Anchor, 1959).
3. Bronislaw Malinowski, *Magic, Science and Religion* (Garden City: Anchor, 1954).
4. Jürgen Moltmann, *The Crucified God*, trans. R. A. Wilson and John Bowden (New York: Harper and Row, 1974).
5. For a somewhat different approach to the dilemma of liberal Christianity cf. John Cobb's *Liberal Christianity at the Crossroads* (Philadelphia: Westminster, 1973).

Chapter 10

Validity and Provisionality

The last several chapters have described the various contexts of theological reflection and the dialectical movement by which a series of contrasting perspectives are brought into mutually informing relation to each other. These discussions severally and together converge toward the question of the validity of theological interpretation. It is to this question and its corollaries that we now turn.

Theological reflection issues in theological judgment. Apart from such issue its dialectic is devoid of direction and purpose. The quest of theology is for a communicable understanding of the significance of the Christian mythos or one of its elements for contemporary human being and becoming. Such understanding is expressed in the form of the judgment: "this is what (or some of what) is meant."

Do such judgments have validity? Is there some means of deciding whether to place confidence in such a judgment? How may we distinguish between more and less valid judgments? Are there ways of testing such judgments? Such questions force themselves upon us with some urgency, for in them we are confronted with a fateful alternative: either there is some possibility of assessing the validity of a theological judgment or the possibility of meaningful public discourse is at an end. The student (and more often than we like to admit, the teacher) of theology may often find herself or himself at the mercy of the last book read, without clear means of assessing the validity of the position therein taken. In a situation in which one's judgment is thus subject to the whims of temporal proximity (the last book) and rhetorical pyrotechnics (it has a nice ring to it), one is apt to lose confidence in the validity of one's own judgment and that of those rascally and contradictory theologians one is reading or, perhaps, conversing with.

In the face of such a failure of nerve theologians and those they influence have frequently attempted to cut the Gordian knot by appeal to some single criterion of validity whereby to separate wheat from chaff.

Protestantism has more than once heard the siren call of biblicism which purports to determine the validity of a theological judgment by the single criterion of its compatibility with Scripture. Now even if we leave aside the problem of the literal incompatibility of perspectives and subsequent assertions in the variety of texts themselves, we are quickly led to see the improbability of this solution. Either we are reduced to the literal repetition of biblical phrases (in which, of course, theology can play no part at all), or the entire problematic of the interpretation of biblical assertions arises. The first possibility has to be rejected since it is itself unbiblical, hence self-contradictory. (That it is unbiblical is clear from the way in which Luke reads Mark, Paul interprets the story of Abraham or Jesus discusses the commandments, to cite only the most obvious examples.) The proposed solution is then but the name of the problem—or that whole host of problems with which this essay has been concerned.

The matter turns out the same when ecclesiastical authority is invoked to settle the problem. Either one must have recourse to univocal pronouncement (as in *ex cathedra* pronouncements) or one has to resort to more complex determinations of the mind of the community. Since, as recent Catholic exegesis of papal pronouncements has shown, even these statements retain ambiguity as to their meaning, we are thrust unremittingly onward in a quest for a measure of validity.

If these two (biblical and ecclesiastical) possibilities for sorting out the problem of validity have been rejected, it is often because they seem to invoke a heteronomous criterion for theological judgment. In their place may be proffered therefore some autonomous criteria for assessing adequacy, e.g., reason. A purely rational criterion, however, can at best tell us whether a position is rational, that is, whether it is free of contradiction and fallacious deduction—it is formal rather than material. One may attempt therefore to combine this with a material criterion. The most rigorous among recent proposals has been that of the verification principle of logical positivism. Despite the valiant attempts of such theologians as Paul van Buren it became clear that this could not work, in part because of what Ian Ramsey has termed the

logical oddity of theoretical assertions—an oddity for which the
first part of this essay has tried to account.

It would be possible to continue this catalogue of possible
simple tests for validity indefinitely. In every case we would
find, I think, that each opens onto a host of issues for which it
has purported to be the solution. Is there then no solution?
Clearly there is no simple one but this need not reduce us to that
frenzy of each one doing his or her own thing which, we are told,
was the punishment inflicted upon Babel.

Each of the foregoing options has had in common a tendency
to confuse validity with certainty. The quest for certainty seems
to be a particularly modern phenomenon. It provides a guiding
theme for philosophy from Descartes to Husserl, from Locke to
Bertrand Russell. The fever for such certainty has clearly infected
theology, at least since the seventeenth century. It is ironic that
the age in which humanity has been most emphasized as norm and
measure is also the one dominated by so egregious a flight from the
conditions of human being as represented by a quest for certainty.
In any case theological judgments, for reasons soon to be mentioned, are never certain; they are never indisputable, final or
absolute.

What we are after here is not an unreasonable certainty but a
reasonable validity. What we need is a way of assessing our own
and one another's judgments to discover whether they are reliable,
trustworthy, adequate or valid. We want to know when we can
place some confidence in our own or another's theological understanding, interpretation, judgment.

If the argument of this essay to this point has merit, then an
answer has already been given to just this sort of question. It
remains now only to be summarized. Our discussion has moved
through a series of contrasting perspectives, each of which polar
contrast has been held together by an inner unity. *The validity of
a theological judgment depends upon its unification of as many of
these contrasts as possible.* This is no arbitrary procedure for, as
I have tried to indicate, each polarity derives its unity-in-contrast
on the one hand from the mythos upon which theology reflects,
and from the condition of our common humanity on the other.
What we are after in theological understanding is the articulation
of the fullest amplitude of intentionality in the mythos, together
with the greatest density and range of our existence in the world.

What these polarities provide, then, are ways of enlarging our understanding of the mythos and our existence, thereby rendering the judgments which articulate that understanding of mythos and existence more valid.

Now the reader will have noticed that this entails the coordination of a number of different perspectives. Theology, like bicycle riding, is largely a matter of coordination. While any detailed analysis of all that must be coordinated in either may disclose byzantine complications, nevertheless each may be done with reasonable grace after a bit of practice. Theology seals itself in a tomb echoing with its own jargon if it does not seek to make it possible for more rather than fewer people to perform its tasks.

Lest the prospect of coordinating so many perspectives threaten to paralyze initiative, let me simply indicate that one does, in practice, work within certain limits. The important thing is to acknowledge and be clear about those limits—thus one has a chance at keeping clear the limit of the validity of one's own or another's particular theological judgment.

The ideal limit of a theological judgment, like that of a judgment in biochemistry or literary criticism, is that it articulates the best available opinion. Now this presupposes first a plurality of opinion and a community of mutual assessment. Like the biochemist and literary critic, the theologian is situated within a community of persons involved in making and evaluating judgments germane to that discipline. Unlike them, however, the community within which this process occurs is for the theologian not restricted to a group of fellow scientists or scholars (though the equivalents of these do create a crucial community). Instead it extends to include all those who understand their existence in the world by virtue of the mythos. That is, the community of theological judgment is that broad community termed the church—and ultimately that still more fractured community called the world.

This leads to the suggestion of a different way of understanding the validity of a theological judgment, not separable from the first, but likewise crucial. Stated succinctly, a theological judgment is valid when it actualizes the Christian mythos. What is meant by this is expressible in the language of the new hermeneutic. The language of the mythos is eventful in character—it is language which expresses an event and which drives toward the happening of that to which it is a reply in the response of the hearer. When the mythos is actualized it means that the event which founded the mythos now founds the existence of the one to whom the mythos is addressed. The quest for understanding is a quest whose banner is "what does this mean?" But the event of understanding is the recognition: "it means me (us)!" One who sought to interpret the mythos now consents to being interpreted by it. The reflection which arose from the symbol returns to the symbol, the symbol which gave expression to and arose from faith, returns to faith—the faith which arose from the address and presence of the sacred returns to that from which it sprang. Theology drives toward proclamation, proclamation to confession. A judgment, therefore, is theologically valid when it is situated along this trajectory.

Now if it be objected that this presupposes the truth of the Christian mythos, then it must certainly be admitted that it does at least suppose, if not *pre*suppose it. A judgment which stands outside the trajectory just described may certainly be a valid judgment—it is simply not a theological judgment. Thus the judgment that the Christian mythos actually speaks of the death of God may be a valid theological judgment, but one which holds that the Christian mythos is utterly without meaning is not a theological judgment. (It may, of course, be a valid judgment of some other sort.)

Our discussion of the validity of theological judgments already anticipates what is to be said of their provisionality. There are several ways of becoming clear about the way in which no theological judgment is reducible to finality. First, theology depends upon the development of skills for the investigation of the import of the constituent ingredients of the mythos. Take biblical scholarship, for example. A shift in the investigatory method may shed fresh light upon a phrase or chain of argument in one of Paul's letters, making it necessary to think through again its meaning. Sometimes a small shift may result in a major transformation in understanding. The recent history of theology is a mine of examples of just this sort of shifting. At the other end of the spectrum a change in our cultural environment may cause some previously important question to fade into the background with a new one coming to the fore to occasion a fresh crisis of interpretation. So the shift in Europe from a mood of cultural optimism to one of cultural pessimism in the period following the First World War, was not without profound influence upon theology. Theology is incorrigibly situated in history—it has no access to an Olympian prospect from which to view calmly the torrents of time. Theological judgments, like the curious beings who beget them, are temporal and mortal.

It should be noted that this judgment is itself both phenomenological and dogmatic. A study of the history of theologians and their judgments discloses their common immersion in time and history. But, as we noted in chapter five, the reality of time and history is a prominent structure of the Christian mythos. Precisely to the extent that theological judgments are responsive to their time, they are responsive to the structure of the Christian mythos. But that they are thus responsive to the historical conditions of existence means that they await and anticipate revision by subsequent judgment answerable in its own way to its own time.

This leads me to say that the impossibility of a final theological judgment is not unrelated to the fact that finality is, in the Christian mythos, reserved not for the past nor for the present, but for the future. The essential corollary to the eschatological structure of the mythos is the provisional character of theological judgments. The attempt to achieve understanding is not only composed of the dialectic of past and present, but, as we have seen, is itself a prolepsis or anticipation of apocalyptic lucidity when "we shall know even as we are known."

The provisionality of a theological judgment need not, indeed must not, nourish timidity. The absence of certitude does not plunge us into enervating uncertainty. In fact, anyone who has read a few pages of Barth, Calvin, Luther, Aquinas, Augustine, Athanasius, or Paul, will see that theology has earned its reputation for being an assertive discipline. This assertiveness does not grow out of a forgetfulness of provisionality. A theological judgment is or entails a judgment about the fundamental significance of human life today. One who speaks to such matters appropriately does so with an assertiveness born of urgency. To state it less rhetorically, a theological judgment stands within the trajectory toward proclamation. Proclamation *asserts* meaning. The assertiveness of a theological judgment is the sign of its standing on the way to proclamation, and is thus one sign of theological validity which is the correlate of theological provisionality.

This anticipates what has thus far been left unsaid, but must now be addressed. For the urgency, passion, and hence assertiveness of theological discourse derive not so much from the "what" of theological reflection as from the "that" to which the mythos refers. In Part III we will have occasion to notice the way in which the seriousness and playfulness of theology derive together from the founding of theological discourse in the givenness of the presence of the sacred.

PART III

THE "THAT" OF
THEOLOGICAL INQUIRY

Chapter 11

Transition to Theology

Thus far our description of theology has remained broadly phenomenological. It has attempted to avoid prejudgment of material or doctrinal content, and has sought rather to indicate what a theological judgment entails. In turning to a discussion of the "that" of theological reflection (a curious locution soon to be explained) we tread perilously close to the actual doing of theology. This is as it should be since an introduction to the doing of theology cannot avoid reaching the point of transition from description to practice. Otherwise our discussions of matters preliminary to theology would endlessly ramify, turning back upon themselves and fail of their avowed intent—namely, to invite you to take up the task.

Thus we might term this last and necessarily brief discussion a transition to theology. Of course, many such transitions have already been announced. In this way the discussion of individual and communal opened upon considerations of ecclesiology, and the discussion of particularity and universality opened upon Christology. As noted, however, in the chapter on faith and reflection there is a certain inevitability in the movement between phenomenological reflection and dogmatic or confessional reflection. Thus this essay, whatever its phenomenological, empirical or descriptive pretentions, is unavoidably informed by a view, however nascent or suppressed, of the meaning or meanings of the Christian mythos. Still, it has seemed useful to avoid taking for granted what still has to be investigated—that is, the meaning of the mythos—thus retaining so far as possible the circumspection appropriate to an introduction.

Here we turn to a consideration of that by which theological reflection is ultimately anchored in being and existence. These are matters which it is customary to deal with in theology under the headings of revelation and faith. Despite the likelihood of driving our phenomenological wagon over a dogmatic cliff it is impossible to change course. For what I have set out to do is to suggest the nature of theology. Theology, however, is incomprehensible apart from its reference, not simply to a "what" but also to a "that."

REVELATION AND FAITH

We have said repeatedly that theology is a reflection upon the Christian mythos. But a mythos is not self-referential. It in turn refers to something outside itself of which it is the expression and interpretation. The activity of the imagination is the symbolic transformation of the given. Thus the dream, image, word, symbol, or mythos is a transformation *of something* which we call its given. *What* the imagination produces is image, symbol, ritual, etc. *That* it produces is, in part, the contribution of its given. Imagination is not *creatio ex nihilo*. This thatness transcends the whatness as the dialectic of the unconscious transcends the dream.

The thatness to which a mythos refers is, you may remember, the entrance of the sacred into the profane. This is what in the phenomenology of religions is called a hierophany. In traditional theology it is called revelation. The given which is transformed into mythos is, in the first place, the self-disclosure or revelation of the sacred. This has a number of important consequences which we must now pursue.

Let us begin by recalling an earlier attempt at designating the meaning of the sacred. The sacred, as Eliade has noted, is that which is perceived to be the most fully and fundamentally real. Whether it be the *mana* of Polynesian lore, the Great Spirit of the American Indian, or the triune God of Christendom, it is that which empowers and thus founds reality (and so is most truly real) to which the mythos refers.

In philosophical theology, therefore, which deploys the categories of ontology, the sacred is thematized as Being-itself, or the ground of being (Tillich), or pure actuality (Aquinas), or Being which empowers and gives being to beings (Heidegger-Macquarrie). This terminology develops the sense of overpowering and overflowing being which is given expression in mythic reference to the sacred. As that which is underived, the sacred is the absolute or ultimate and thus not reducible to some other region of experience. One may also speak here of the experience of transcendence

—that is, of that which is other than and more than the human world.

In a somewhat different view Rudolph Otto, in an early treatment of the phenomenology of religion, employs the term "The Holy" to designate what we are here calling the sacred.[1] In this way the sense of mystery, awesomeness, eerieness and fascination is raised prominently into focus.

All of these terms serve to expand and enhance the connotation of sacred. They are certainly not meant to be a covert doctrine of God. They point to the that of theology without yet specifying it.

Now as I have maintained from early on, the sacred is not given to or through the mythos simply in itself. The given of the mythos is not the sacred as such, but the sacred in juxtaposition, apposition, conjunction with the world or some prominent feature of it. This, as Eliade indicates, entails a *coincidentia oppositorum*. The togetherness of contraries, which has been the structural principle of the second part of this essay, is founded in this primordial intersection. This is the root of all paradox in religious and (hence) theological language.

If we were to leave it at this we would still not have given an account of revelation in the religious sense. What thrusts religion away from whatever possibility of disinterestedness and objectivity there may be in these matters for philosophical inquiry, is that the revelation is directed at or toward us. The sacred does not found *a* world through its presence, not even *the* world, but *our* world. Revelation is indissolubly *pro nobis*—it concerns, has to do with, is directed toward, us. If we are to speak here of ultimacy then we should speak of "that which concerns us ultimately." (Tillich). If in wooing the favor of various schools of metaphysics, theology has forgotten this, then it has been reminded of it again in its conversations with existential modes of thought. This is the reason that the polarities of theological reflection have been discussed here in relation both to the mythos and human existence generally.

To this point we have filled out the reference to the "that" which grounds theology with an initial designation of the sacred which intersects our world in such a way as to offer itself to us. The given of the mythos is the sacred giving itself to us in our world.

The *pro nobis* character of revelation indicates its inseparability from faith. Faith, as is often said, is the response to revelation. Apart from faith revelation does not have a *pro nobis* character and thus is not revelatory. Faith therefore as the response to revelation is equally its necessary correlate:

Thus it would seem that we might just as easily have to designate faith as the "that" of theological reflection. It would seem to make perfectly good sense to say that that which is expressed in the mythos, and thus that which is its given, is faith.

At this point we join up with a theological dispute which has, in its most recent form, threatened to divide the world of Protestant theology into warring camps. It is the dispute between Barth and Bultmann. Taking the *pro nobis* character of revelation as his starting point, Bultmann emphasizes the necessary correlate of faith. Faith, or more adequately, existence in faith, thus becomes the grounding of theological reflection. The mythos is the expression of existence in faith, and despite its encrustations with elements of an ancient world view, may still be (with a little demytholog-izing) the adequate and necessary expression of that faith. More recently Gerhard Ebeling has ably seconded this insistence upon theology's grounding in faith.[2]

Barth protests in effect that this bids fair to reduce theology to the level of preoccupation with one's existential temperature (a kind of sophisticated navel-gazing). Faith, like love, preoccupied with itself utterly corrupts itself. One is reminded here of Freud's analysis of narcissism, or Luther's definition of sin as *cor curvam in se*: the heart turned in upon itself. Theology then must be first and last concerned with revelation.

Now this dispute is capable of and has received sophisticated and detailed elaboration. It is mentioned here to indicate how quickly an innocuous looking juxtaposition of revelation and faith opens into full blown theological controversy. For our purposes it is sufficient to notice two things: first, that revelation seems to have a logical, chronological, and ontological priority in comparison with faith. Yet they are inseparably related. Revelation is *pro nobis* (Barth too may write of *The Humanity of God*), and faith is necessarily *coram deo* (living out of and in the presence of the sacred reality to which it is but the response).

Theology can give up neither the priority of revelation nor the inseparable relation between it and faith. Thereby is theology anchored in being and existence. Apart from reference to the sacred and thus to ultimacy, theology severs itself from its foundation and becomes weightless. Apart from its grounding in faith and thereby existence, theology evaporates into aimless speculation. We will return to this consideration in speaking of the seriousness of theology.

"THAT" AND "WHAT"

First, however, it is necessary to notice a certain dubiousness about the way we have come. We have been considering the "that" apart from the "what," the given apart from its symbolic transformation into mythos. Actually, the what has been there all the time, but rendered tacit in order to focus upon the that. This may serve the purpose of preparing the way for a discussion of their connection. If we, for the moment, take revelation as the given and thus the that of theological reflection, then we must say that it is inseparable from the what or symbolic content and structure of the mythos. Apart from this content the given is not given at all, but withheld in silence. We have the possibility of speaking of this given without introducing the content of the mythos only through abstraction from the mythos or from the religious imagination. But the mythos, apart from reference to the revelation of the sacred, is but an idle tale and therefore not a mythos at all. The "whatness" severed from the "thatness" is loosed from ontological moorings and cast adrift, perchance to be salvaged and placed in a museum for wrecked relics.

Revelation, then, is not altogether reducible to a content of revelation. The that transcends the what to which it is, however, inseparably linked. Lest that seem improbable, consider the following parallel. Who you are is not separable from who you disclose yourself to be in word and deed. Yet who you are is not exhausted by what you say and do. Therein lies, for example, the possibility of growth, conscience, and alteration. Your "thatness" transcends your "whatness." This is all the more true in the relation between the event of revelation and the mythos since 1) the sacred transcends the world and the mythos is a part of the world and 2) the event of revelation in the Christian mythos points not to itself but to a future revelation. The eschatological structure of the mythos means that revelation is more like a promise and a down payment than it is like a final manifestation. The event of revelation is thus not contained in but contains the mythos.

The matter stands similarly with faith. It is possible to discriminate two dimensions of faith which we may label trust and conviction. I maintained earlier (chapter six) that they are to be held together. Trust is that which corresponds to revelation, conviction corresponds to the mythos.

If for a moment, we focus attention upon faith as trust, then we may describe it, provisionally, as the resonation of the subject to revelation. Tillich explores the ontological nuance of this relationship by speaking of the grounding of existence in Being-itself or the absolute awareness of the unconditioned. Schleiermacher in quasi-aesthetic categories speaks here of the feeling of absolute dependence. Various kinds of mysticism attempt to bring this intimate relation to expression by referring to the oneness of *atman* and Brahman (Hinduism) or the identification of the soul with the all-encompassing being of God (Eckhart). When this relationship is made absolute and transformed into a soteriological principle, the consequence, most rigorously explored by some kinds of Buddhism, is identification by way of sheer negation—the speechless Nothingness of being corresponding to the emptying of consciousness of all experience or awareness—and thus *Nirvana.* Here thatness is severed from whatness and thus falls into silence.

The suspicion which Christianity harbors of all mysticism is grounded in the indissoluble connection of thatness with whatness. For faith this means that trust is wed to conviction. In conviction faith comes to speech and thus is communicated to awareness. Apart from this, faith cannot be communicated to the other and thus loses its character as social and communal (and therefore human).

Yet a very delicate balance must be maintained here, for if faith is simply and without remainder identified with belief, then its loses its relation to revelation. It becomes one form or another of those ideologies which constantly threaten to destroy faith: biblic*ism*, dogmat*ism*, fundamental*ism*, literal*ism*, confessional*ism*. The "true believer" is thereby the prototype of the "unbeliever." Idolatry in religious practice or in theological reflection is the confusion of the penultimate with the ultimate, the what with the that.

Only on the basis of the possibility of distinguishing between the that and the what does the development of the Judeo-Christian tradition become intelligible. One example may be of assistance here. Let us suppose, as I do, that the expectation of the imminent cataclysmic occurrence of the end of time was a fundamental conviction of the early Christian community—a conviction deriving

at least in part from Jesus' own preaching, and forming
the basis for the initial assessment of the significance of his fate.
This conviction still provides the basic horizon within which the
elements of Paul's theology cohere. But the cataclysm did not
occur. This leads some to suppose a crisis of faith. There is,
however, no evidence of a threatened collapse of faith—instead the
conviction is slowly reinterpreted. It is this process of reinterpre-
tation which eventuates in the classical creedal formulations of the
person of Christ. This example does not stand alone, since the
history of Israel is a series of such reinterpretations. But it may
stand for all such examples since it suggests the close connection
between theology and the eschatological structure by which that
revelation transcends mythos, and faith transcends conviction.
This transcendence is the driving wedge which impels faith toward
reflection. The difference between conviction and trust makes
reflection possible, but the necessity of faith's expression in conviction makes reflection necessary.

We are thus returned to the intimate connection between trust
and conviction, and thus, to the inseparability in distinction obtaining
between the that and the what, the given and the symbol, revelation
and mythos. Existence and reality are mediated only through the
symbol. In the symbol (so long as it symbolizes) these are given
to reflection. Reflection then is proximately a reflection upon the
symbol through which alone it has access to reality. The symbol
makes thought possible, but through the disjunction (by transformation) of symbol and reality it also propels reflection. How, then,
one may rightly ask, does reflection know that there is a difference
between the symbol and the reality if reality is mediated only
through the symbol (and thus may not be compared directly to it)?
Only insofar and to the extent that the difference is inscribed in the
symbol itself. An example of the way in which this difference is
present in the Christian mythos is its eschatological structure. In
pointing to the future as the locus of revelation the mythos distinguishes itself from that to which it points. The phrase of
Käsemann that "apocalyptic is the Mother of theology"[3] designates
not only the temporal and causal priority of the eschatological
structure of the mythos to theology, but also serves to designate the
ground of the possibility of distinguishing through the mythos itself
the that of revelation (and thus of faith) from the what of the
mythos (and thus of conviction) without destroying their unity.

We may summarize this discussion of the relation of the mythos to revelation by stressing the indirectness of theological reflection. Theology, as these last remarks should have made tolerably clear, does not possess its given. It can claim no direct access to that which gives it sense and significance. Thus it cannot claim to have its given as an object for possession and dialectical manipulation. It is removed from immediacy in at least three ways.

First, theology is a reflection upon the mythos. This means that the proximate grounding of reflection is in that which forever eludes its comprehension. A mythos, remember, is not an allegory, and thus not susceptible of total reduction to conceptual clarity. The reflection which seeks to interpret the symbol must finally consent (though in its own interest in understanding and thus not heteronomously) to being interpreted by the symbol. Theological reflection is inextricably bound to its other—the mythos.

Second, the mythos is a symbolic transformation of the given designated as the manifestation of the sacred. While the mythos mediates its given, it is not identical with and so does not possess that given. In absolutizing itself the mythos loses its identity as mythos and becomes ideology—the distortion rather than the mediation of reality. Thereby is established the ontological difference whereby the mythos is founded on but not identical with its revelatory given.

Third, the difference between the given and its expression is inscribed ineluctably in the eschatological character of the Christian mythos. However, a mythos may lapse into forgetfulness of the ontological difference. Here the transformation of an ontological into an eschatological difference prods that forgetfulness to awaken it from dogmatic slumber. For every dogmatism and biblicism which would attempt to freeze the given of the mythos at some point in "the dark backward and abysm of time," there is the announcement of the mythos itself: "he is not here. . . he is going before you."

Thus the given of theology is articulated upon a threefold absence and the last of these is the greatest among them. All talk therefore of theology's given must bear the imprint and imprimatur of this absence. To speak of that which is given is to speak of that which is also withheld and therefore not to be grasped, dominated, bound, or finalized by a system or institution.

Theology has need therefore of constant vigilance against all pretensions to directness and immediacy. It is perennially seduced by the siren call of unmediated presence. In philosophy the pretensions of Idealism, the intuitional phenomenology of Husserl, and the temptations of primary thinking derived from Heidegger, all are allegations of immediacy, which if taken into theological reflection, must defect from the very beginning the integrity of theological discourse. No less deadly are those forms of dogmatism, ecclesiasticism or biblicism which foster the collapse of trust into conviction, of revelation into the mythos. This vigilance is but the reflective (and reflected) counterpart to all prophetic discourse which shatters adhesion to absolutized institutions and histories to make way for that which ever evades their entombing grasp. Prophetic discourse anticipates and gives birth to apocalyptic. It is not without significance, that the word apocalyptic has for us become so closely associated with the most vigorous form of reference to the future. The word itself simply means revelation, but revelation points not to its past but to its future and thus is apocalyptic.

The indirectness which is congenital to theology determines the mode of its reflection to be dialectical. This insight has governed the discussion of the character of theology in Part II. There we noted repeatedly that theological reflection consists in the movement between contrasting perspectives. These perspectives are not reducible to one another, nor is the tension between them soluable to a "middle road." Rather, the movement between them is, as Ray Hart notes in a similar connection, an open-ended spiral.[4] No theological judgment is a resolution of this dialectic, but is instead a pause to report on movement thus far. Its validity consists in its holding together of contraries themselves derived from the mythos. But the resistance of these polarities to resolution (itself founded on the indirectness and non-finality of the mythos), is what makes a valid judgment also a provisional one. Theology, like the faith it mirrors, is a pilgrimage whose destination it does not itself build.

In theology itself the problematic we have been circumscribing is discussed in terms of the dogmatic (i.e., derived from the mythos) category of the Word of God. Under this heading the relationships among revelation, mythos (Scripture and tradition), proclamation, and theology receive their specifically theological focus. In discussing these issues from a different perspective (dominated by the category of the imagination) I have by no means tackled, let alone resolved, the issues which engage the attention of theology under the heading of a doctrine of the Word of God. Rather I have sought to indicate how the issues arise.

SERIOUSNESS AND PLAYFULNESS

In thinking about the indirectness of theological reflection, it is important not to lose sight of its relation to that which it cannot possess. It is this relation by way of indirection which gives theology its seriousness. It is preoccupied with the meaning of human existence as that existence is illumined by (and illumines) the Christian mythos, and as it is founded in the ultimate reality of the sacred. Such matters are not frivolous for they have to do with the meaning by which we live.

Apart from its meaningful patterning by symbol, being sinks into nothingness and the abyss yawns hideously. Without symbols we have no access to reality, not even to that fragment of reality which is our existence. The collapse of our symbols entails the amputation of our existence and constriction of our access to reality. Apart from the mediative function of symbol the horizon of meaning within which we have our being fades into the ironic grin (and grimace) of absurdity.

Theology contributes to that humane quest for meaning which is the driving force of culture, such partial and fragmentary glimpses of meaning as it discerns in the myths and symbols of faith. In its inevitable movement from particularity to universality it contributes what it may to the healing of those divisions which so fragment and specialize our languages, disciplines, and perspectives as to sever us from community and condemn us all to sectarian isolation.

In a culture given over to the manipulation of objects in the ascendancy of technique over meaning, theology is compelled to speak of the healing which comes through the symbol, of the meanings manifest in the imagination, of the participation mediated by the image. It is not alone in this vocation—others among the humanities share in its labors. But theology has special need to quicken the sense for the image, for it is reflection upon a mythos.

To this urgency, which couples our labors with those who would humanize our society and purify its perception, there is another which engenders its own seriousness. Theology cannot survive and give up the distinction between authentic and heretical meanings. Once this is lost the passion for truth decays and with it the contours of meaning. Truth is not a property of ideas alone. If it were, then no urgent problem would arise with falsity. It is a quality of life. Meanings gone astray lead lives astray. The reflection upon meaning in the quest for understanding is not an idle pastime of a leisure class but fraught with the twin alternatives: to enhance or to distort human being. Only when this is seen can one understand the passion with which theological controversy has been laden in times of decisive formulations of faith's convictions. What was at stake at Nicea and Chalcedon for those who participated (if not for us) was the fundamental structure of the meanings by which human existence was to be guided.

The modern age has been populated by a jostling series of contending ideologies. In their wake there is strewn the carnage of deformed and truncated lives. A theology which knows and practices the difference between the absolute and the institutions or beliefs by which it enters into our experience is in a position to contribute to the exposure of such murderous falsehoods. But not before it has turned its critical gaze upon itself and the community it serves. The relativism into which we have been plunged has produced a church that no longer knows what it is about (unless it be institutional self-preservation). In the church, as elsewhere, the malaise which falls upon those who have lost their zest for truth is breeding, as it has in the past, the champions of immediacy who absolutize their pet preoccupation into a rule of faith. An authentic dogmatic theology must do battle today, as in other days, against every dogmatism which purports to possess (in Bible or ecstasy or institution) its own ground.

There is, then, reason for theology to be assertive and serious. But this must not for a moment be permitted to obscure the essential playfulness of theology. Theology is not the deadly serious business of creating meaning but the merriment of conveying it. The playfulness of theology is rooted in the givenness of meaning, meaning which is granted gratuitously and altogether in advance of whatever merits may accrue to reflection. The givenness which theology acknowledges is the gracious *pro nobis* of revelation, not a heteronomous law devised for the imprisonment of the human heart and mind. Existence, sometimes, is represented to us under the guise of the paucity of being. With chaos threatening on every hand and existence threatening to sink into non-being, modern and primitive people alike might have reason to regard life as a dull and desperate routine of getting enough meaning or food or what have you to get by on. This is existence marked by the paucity of being driven by the law of the kingdom of necessity. Then there is religion—human enough to fall into and inflict any of those inhuman and dehumanizing practices of our common humanity—yet pointing, sometimes obliviously, to a different picture of our world. The world is transfigured by the sign of the sacred, the presence of which is the excess of being. The world, or that space of it opened up by the presence of the sacred, becomes the kingdom of freedom.

The playfulness of theology is grounded in the assurance that its labors are permitted and are, like all labors, justified not by their merit but by grace. The eschatological character of the Christian mythos comes once more into play here. The recollection of the paradigmatic events of the past as promise manifests, as has been noted before, the present as the time of love. Most fundamentally love is not required but permitted. That is, preoccupation with oneself and one's own meaning is rendered unnecessary by the prevenience and promise of grace. The sphere of Christian faith and action stand therefore, as Herbert Braun has noted, under the sign of the "I may" rather than "I ought."[5] Metaphors of obligation, Kant to the contrary notwithstanding, are secondary to metaphors of permission. Theology, which has the task of bringing this structure to understanding and expression, does so in such a way as to reflect the permissiveness of revelation in the playfulness of speech. This it does in several ways, some of which may be briefly indicated.

The dialectical structure of theological reflection is itself an exemplification of this playfulness, both in its avoidance of strident one-sidedness and in the spiraling dance-like movement of understanding. Provisionality as well liberates theology from stridency (without eliminating authentic assertiveness) and creates the space for that humour which characterizes the theology, for example, of Karl Barth. The movement toward universality of scope provides some of the best range for playfulness, where the attention is focused not simply on the pressing questions of the day, but ranges into intricate issues of nuance whose practical relevance is often, though not always, at the vanishing point. The example by which a bourgeois temper dismissed scholastic theology was the question: how many angels can dance on the head of a pin? One may focus on the wildly irrelevant nature of such questions in dismay or in delight at their intricacy, ingenuity, and playfulness. In a cultural ethos strangling upon its own efficiency, practicality, and relevancy, a theology which can entertain questions about the dancing of angels can scarcely be all bad.

This leads me to comment briefly on the virtues of irrelevance. I have argued and believe that theology may make a significant contribution to the urgent tasks of creating a more humane culture and society. That may be the relevance of theology. But theology cannot permit its horizon to be restricted to this relevance, still less by the habitual or ideological ways of determining relevance. So, for example, it cannot appropriate the standards of an objectivistic and technocentric culture as determinative of its style or content— as determining what it may and may not say. As great a danger, however, lurks in the possible surrender of theology's scope and reflective dialectic to the dictates of a counter-cultural aversion to reflection and a preoccupation with the non-verbal. Theology, which entails a confrontation of past and present, phenomenological and dogmatic, will always stand in some tension to, and therefore apparent irrelevance for, both cultures and counter-cultures. This irrelevance can, of course, issue in prophetic denunciations of a culture, but it may also manifest itself in an apparent oblivion to pressing matters which is the essence of play.

The playfulness of theology, then, is not in opposition to its seriousness, but in opposition to every form of absolute seriousness which implicitly or explicitly denies the graciousness and gracefulness of life. Thus the sternest rebukes of dogmatic theology are properly directed against those perspectives which in some way or other undermine the graciousness of existence and reality as given in the gracious giving of the sacred. Thus all those doctrines by which the givenness of grace is disfigured by treating it as a possession (biblicism, spiritualism), as a reward (legalism, moralism), or as an esoterica (gnosticism, fundamentalism), especially as these pose as representative of Christian faith (but also their secular and even philosophical equivalents), are those against which the vigor of theology's dogmatic seriousness is properly turned. In this way the seriousness serves precisely as guardian of the space of playful response to, expression and anticipation of, the appearance of grace. The subordination of seriousness to playfulness parallels the subordination of obligation to permission, of reflection to imagination.

The consideration of the seriousness and playfulness of theology

may be joined together under the rubric of love. The present, I have suggested, is figured as the time of love, and the tasks of theology are situated within that time, shaped as it is by memory and anticipation. The gathering together of seriousness (fidelity) and playfulness (delight) in theology is simply the imitation of love. Theological reflection is always reflection on behalf of, as has been noted before. It is reflection on behalf of a community, on behalf of tradition, on behalf of a world. In this, as in its refusal to have that which is its source at its own disposal, issuing both in seriousness and in playfulness, theology is a labor of love.

These considerations serve to amplify the significance of theology's reference to a givenness present in, yet transcending the content of the mythos. Theology, as I have said, is made both possible and necessary by this togetherness of and distinction between the thatness and the whatness of its reflections. I have attempted to keep this discussion to the near side of the phenomenological-dogmatic polarity. The issues to which I have referred are but the schematic outline of what in theology would be treated under the doctrine of the Word of God. Any movement beyond these indications, in the way of their phenomenological and dogmatic amplification, would be to move this essay within the precincts of theological discourse, to which I have sought to provide an introduction and invitation. The prologue, which anticipates the drama it precedes, must therefore close, as all the best prologues do with the invitation—let the play begin.

NOTES

1. Rudolph Otto, *The Idea of the Holy*, trans. John W. Harvey (London: Oxford University Press, 1923).
2. Gerhard Ebeling's disagreement with Barth at this point is argued in his essay "Jesus and Faith" in *Word and Faith*, trans. James W. Leitch (Philadelphia: Fortress Press, 1963), pp. 201 ff.
3. Cf. Ernst Käsemann, "The Beginnings of Christian Theology" in *New Testament Questions of Today* (Philadelphia: Fortress Press, 1969), pp. 82–107.
4. Ray L. Hart, *Unfinished Man and the Imagination* (New York: Herder and Herder, 1968), pp. 60–1.
5. Herbert Braun, "The Problem of New Testament Theology" *The Bultmann School of Biblical Interpretation: New Directions*, Vol I of *Journal for Theology and the Church* (New York: Harper & Row, 1965).

INDEX OF NAMES

Altizer, Thomas, 62, 131
Anselm, 94
Aquinas, Thomas, 68, 69, 79n., 163, 167
Athanasius, 163
Auerbach, Erich, 71
Augustine, 69, 132, 163

Barfield, Owen, 12, 16, 36, 44, 138n.
Barth, Karl, 4, 5, 9, 38, 39, 57, 61–62, 72, 80–81, 96, 97, 99, 116, 120, 135, 141, 163, 169, 177
Berger, Peter, 138
Bloch, Ernst, 35, 78
Boers, Hendrick, 105n.
Bonhoeffer, Dietrich, 4, 61–62, 96, 99, 102, 132
Braun, Herbert, 70, 177
Brown, Norman O., 16
Brunner, Emil, 99
Buber, Martin, 139
Bultmann, Rudolph, 47–48, 65, 72, 76n., 97, 104, 116, 125, 169
Bunyan, John, 69
Buri, Fritz, 48, 79n.

Calvin, John, 102, 113–14, 163
Cassirer, Ernst, 19–20, 22, 34, 137
Cobb, John, 100, 156n.
Coleridge, Samuel Taylor, 11
Comte, Auguste, 12
Congar, Yves, 118n.
Cox, Harvey, 62n., 131n.

Descartes, Réné, 12, 16, 160
Dilthey, Wilhelm, 122, 125
Dunne, John, 131n.
Durkheim, Emile, 39–42, 50, 52, 140–41

Ebeling, Gerhard, 62n., 120, 128, 169
Ebner, Ferdinand, 139
Eckhart, Meister, 171
Eddy, Mary Baker, 69
Eliade, Mircea, 42–43, 51, 130, 153, 167, 168
Eliot, T. S., 117
Ellul, Jacques, 14

Ferré, Frederic, 93n.
Feuerbach, Ludwig, 9, 38–40, 44
Freud, Sigmund, 26–28, 29, 35, 39, 85, 130, 131, 139, 169

Gadamer, Hans-Georg, 122, 125, 128
Gloege, Gerhard, 112n.
Gogarten, Friedrich, 62

Hare, R. M., 92–93
Hart, Ray, 23n., 174
Hartshorne, Charles, 100
Harvey, Van, 74n., 108
Heidegger, Martin, 19, 34, 100, 101, 122, 125, 130, 167, 174
Hegel, G. W. F., 14, 47, 102
Herder, J. G., 11
Hirsh, E. D., 125n.
Hoffmann, Manfred, 124n.